EASY
FRENCH
COOKING

EASY FRENCH COOKING

Hélène Molard

Larousse & Co., Inc., New York

© 1985 by Libraire Larousse USA Inc.

First published in the United States and Canada
by Larousse & Co., Inc.,
572 Fifth Avenue, New York, N.Y.10036

ISBN 0-88332-444-X

Library of Congress No. 84-52829

Printed and bound in Spain by Graficromo, S.A., Cordoba

Notes

It is important to follow *either* the metric, imperial *or* the American measures when using the recipes in this book.

American terminology within recipes is indicated by the use of brackets in both the list of ingredients and in the methods.

American measures which follow metric and imperial measures within the recipe methods are preceded by the term 'us'.

All spoon measures are level.

Each dish will serve four people, unless otherwise indicated.

Flour is plain (all-purpose) and sugar is granulated, unless otherwise indicated.

Acknowledgements

The publishers would like to thank the following organizations for supplying colour photographs:

Food and Wine from France (page 1, page 2, page 14, page 20, page 35, page 53, page 61, page 63, page 65)

John West Foods Ltd (page 25)

Moulinex Ltd (page 69)

National Dairy Council (page 59)

Potato Marketing Board (page 49, page 50, page 51)

Seafish Industry Authority (page 19)

Photographs on pages 6, 8, 15, 17, 39, 43, 54, 56, 57, 67, 73, 74
© Orbis-Verlag für Publizistik 1985

CONTENTS

Soups and First Courses   7

Fish and Shellfish   18

Meat and Poultry   28

Eggs and Cheese   44

Vegetables and Salads   49

Desserts   57

Baking   67

Sauces and Other Basics   75

Index   80

SOUPS AND FIRST COURSES

Crème Vichyssoise

Metric/imperial		American
25g/1 oz	butter	2 tablespoons
275g/10 oz	leeks, white parts only, chopped	2½ cups
	1 medium onion, chopped	
	2 large potatoes, peeled and diced	
200ml/⅓ pint	chicken stock	⅞ cup
	salt	
150ml/¼ pint	milk	⅔ cup
200ml/⅓ pint	single (light) cream	⅞ cup
	Tabasco (hot pepper) sauce	
	GARNISH chopped chives	

Melt the butter in a pan, and cook the leeks and onion until soft. Add the potatoes with the chicken stock and salt, and simmer for about 35 minutes until all the vegetables are cooked.

Pass the vegetables and liquid through a sieve, or process in a blender or food processor. Add the milk and 150ml/¼ pint/⅔ US cup cream, then bring the soup back to the boil. Sieve or blend again, then add a dash of Tabasco (hot pepper) sauce and the remaining cream. Chill until ready to serve, then garnish with chives.

Pistou

(Garlic Soup)

SERVES 4–6

Metric/imperial		American
1.2 litres/2 pints	water	5 cups
100g/4 oz	potatoes, peeled and diced	⅔ cup
	2 tomatoes, de-seeded and chopped	
450g/1 lb	French (green) beans, chopped	1 lb
	4 onions, chopped	
	2 green peppers, de-seeded and chopped	
225g/8 oz	vegetable marrow (squash), de-seeded and chopped	1½ cups
	salt, freshly ground pepper	
50g/2 oz	vermicelli	½ cup
	3 cloves garlic, crushed	
2 × 5ml spoons/ 2 teaspoons	olive oil	2 teaspoons
½ × 2.5ml spoon/ ¼ teaspoon	dried basil	¼ teaspoon

Put the water into a saucepan and heat to boiling point. Add the vegetables, then simmer for 15–20 minutes. Add the salt, pepper and vermicelli, and cook for a further 8–10 minutes.

Pound the garlic with the oil and basil. Add a little hot soup, then return the mixture to the pan, stir well and heat through for 2–3 minutes.

Serve with grated Gruyère cheese.

Crème Vichyssoise

Soupe à L'Oignon Gratinée

Potage à la Crecy

(Carrot Soup)

Metric/imperial		American
15g/½ oz	butter	1 tablespoon
450g/1 lb	carrots, chopped	1 lb
	1 medium onion, chopped	
	2 sticks celery, chopped	
	½ small turnip or swede, chopped	
600ml/1 pint	stock	2½ cups
	bouquet garni	
	a little yeast extract	
	lemon juice	
	salt, freshly ground pepper	
150ml/¼ pint	milk	⅔ cup
	cornflour (cornstarch)	
	extra milk	

Melt the butter in a deep saucepan, add the vegetables, and fry gently for 5–10 minutes without browning them. Add the stock, bouquet garni, yeast extract and lemon juice, and season to taste. Heat to boiling point, then simmer gently until the vegetables are quite soft. Do not overcook them.

Remove the bouquet garni, and pass the vegetables and liquid through a fine sieve, or process in a blender or food processor. Add the milk, then measure the soup, and return it to a clean pan. For each 600ml/1 pint/2½ US cups puréed soup, blend 4 × 5ml spoons/4 teaspoons cornflour (cornstarch) with a little extra milk. Stir it into the soup, then bring to the boil, stirring all the time, and cook for 5 minutes. Season to taste.

Serve with croûtons.

Soupe à L'Oignon Gratinée

(Onion Soup)

SERVES 6

Metric/imperial		American
50g/2 oz	fat bacon, rinds removed and chopped	¼ cup
	6 medium onions, thinly sliced	
1 × 2.5ml spoon/ ½ teaspoon	French (Dijon-style) mustard	½ teaspoon
900ml/1½ pints	consommé (page 10)	3¾ cups
150ml/¼ pint	dry white wine	⅔ cup
	salt, freshly ground pepper	
	6 slices French bread	
	butter	
50g/2 oz	Gruyère or Parmesan cheese, grated	½ cup

Heat the bacon gently in a deep saucepan until the fat runs freely. Add the onions, and fry slowly until golden-brown. Stir in the mustard, consommé and wine, heat to boiling point, then simmer gently for 1 hour or until the onions are quite soft. Season to taste. Toast the bread, spread with butter, then with the grated cheese.

Pour the soup into individual ovenproof soup bowls, float a slice of toast on each, and brown the cheese under the grill (broiler).

Crème Dubarry

(Cream of Cauliflower Soup)

Metric/imperial		American
	1 large cauliflower, divided into florets	
25g/1 oz	butter	2 tablespoons
25g/1 oz	flour	$\frac{1}{4}$ cup
900ml/1$\frac{1}{2}$ pints	chicken stock	3$\frac{3}{4}$ cups
300ml/$\frac{1}{2}$ pint	milk	1$\frac{1}{4}$ cups
	salt	
	ground nutmeg	
	1 egg yolk	
5 × 5ml spoons/ 5 teaspoons	single (light) cream	5 teaspoons

Blanch the cauliflower for about 10 minutes in boiling water, then drain. Pass about two-thirds of it through a sieve, or process in a blender or food processor.

Melt the butter in a pan, stir in the flour, and cook for 1 minute. Stir in the stock, then cook for 7 minutes, stirring all the time. Add the puréed cauliflower and the milk, and bring back to the boil. Season to taste with salt and nutmeg, then remove from the heat. Whisk together the egg yolk and cream, and stir into the hot soup without letting it boil. Add the remaining cauliflower florets, and serve at once.

Soupe à L'Oseille

(Cream of Sorrel Soup)

SERVES 4–6

Metric/imperial		American
25g/1 oz	butter	2 tablespoons
225g/8 oz	sorrel leaves, shredded	$\frac{1}{2}$ lb
100g/4 oz	lettuce, shredded	1$\frac{1}{2}$ cups
	1 small onion, chopped	
225g/8 oz	potatoes, peeled and sliced	$\frac{1}{2}$ lb
1.2 litres/2 pints	water	5 cups
	salt, freshly ground pepper	
4–8 × 15ml spoons/ 4–8 tablespoons	single (light) cream	5–9 tablespoons

Melt the butter in a deep saucepan, add the vegetables, and fry gently for 10 minutes. Heat the water to boiling point, add to the pan, and simmer for 10–15 minutes.

Pass the soup through a fine sieve, or process in a blender or food processor, then return it to the pan. Season to taste, bring the soup back to the boil, then add the cream. Serve at once.

Soupe à L'Oseille

Bouillabaisse

(Mixed Fish Soup)

Metric/imperial		American
10 × 5ml spoons/ 10 teaspoons	olive oil	10 teaspoons
300g/11 oz	tomatoes, skinned and sliced	scant ¾ lb
100g/4 oz	leeks, sliced	1 cup
225g/8 oz	potatoes, peeled and sliced	½ lb
100g/4 oz	onions, chopped	1 cup
25g/1 oz	red pepper, de-seeded and chopped	¼ cup
225g/8 oz	white fish fillets, cubed and small shellfish, mixed	½ lb
150ml/¼ pint	Muscadet	⅔ cup
1.2 litres/2 pints	water	5 cups
50g/2 oz	concentrated tomato purée (paste)	¼ cup
	1 chicken stock (bouillon) cube	
	bouquet garni	
	fresh fennel leaves	
	1 clove of garlic, crushed	
	salt, freshly ground pepper	
	GARNISH chopped parsley	

Heat the oil in a large saucepan, add the vegetables, cover and cook gently for 7–8 minutes; do not let them colour. Add the fish and shellfish, and fry for 3 minutes, turning them over to firm the surface. Pour in the wine, water and tomato purée (paste), and crumble in the stock (bouillon) cube. Add the bouquet garni, fennel leaves and garlic, and season to taste. Heat to boiling point, and simmer for 20 minutes, then discard the bouquet garni. Pour into a soup tureen and sprinkle with the chopped parsley.

Consommé Royale

SERVES 4–6

Metric/imperial		American
100g/4 oz	lean shin (bottom round) of beef, finely shredded	½ cup
150ml/¼ pint	water	⅔ cup
	1 small onion, sliced	
	1 small carrot, sliced	
	1 small stick of celery, sliced	
1.5 litres/2½ pints	beef stock	6¼ cups
	bouquet garni	
	salt, freshly ground pepper	
	4 white peppercorns	
	white and crushed shell of 1 egg	
	ROYALE CUSTARD 1 egg yolk	
	salt, freshly ground pepper	
1 × 15ml spoon/ 1 tablespoon	milk	1 tablespoon

Soak the meat in the water for 15 minutes, then put into a deep saucepan with the rest of the ingredients, adding the egg white and shell last. Heat slowly to simmering point, whisking all the time, until a froth rises to the surface. Remove the whisk, then cover and simmer very gently for 1½–2 hours. Do not allow to boil or the froth will break up and cloud the consommé. Strain slowly into a basin through muslin (cheesecloth) or a scalded jelly bag. If necessary, strain the consommé again. Re-heat, and season to taste.

Meanwhile, prepare the Royale Custard. Mix together the egg yolk, seasoning and milk, then strain into a small greased basin (heatproof mixing bowl), and cover with buttered greaseproof (waxed) paper or foil. Stand the basin in a pan of simmering water, and steam the custard for about 8 minutes or until firm. Leave until cold, then turn out. Cut into thin slices and then into tiny fancy shapes. Rinse the custard shapes in hot water, then drain.

Add the custard garnishes to the consommé just before serving.

Consommé Royale

Champignons à la Grecque

(Marinated Mushrooms)

Metric/imperial		American
450g/1 lb	mushrooms	1 lb
	SAUCE	
4 × 15ml spoons/ 4 tablespoons	olive oil	5 tablespoons
2 × 15ml spoons/ 2 tablespoons	lemon juice	3 tablespoons
150ml/¼ pint	water	⅔ cup
	1 bay leaf	
	1 sprig of thyme	
1 × 2.5ml spoon/ ½ teaspoon	coriander seeds, crushed	½ teaspoon
	1 clove of garlic, crushed	
	salt, freshly ground pepper	
450g/1 lb	tomatoes, skinned and chopped	1 lb

Prepare the sauce first. Put the oil, lemon juice, water, bay leaf, thyme, coriander seeds, garlic and seasoning into a saucepan, and heat to boiling point. Add the tomatoes, and cook, uncovered, over moderate heat for 25 minutes.

Pour the hot sauce over the mushrooms, and leave to cool. Remove the bay leaf and thyme before serving.

Salade Niçoise

SERVES 4–6

Metric/imperial		American
	1 large lettuce	
225g/8 oz	cooked French (green) beans	½ lb
	2 hard-boiled eggs, quartered	
	3 tomatoes, skinned and quartered	
	1 clove of garlic, crushed	
225g/8 oz	canned tuna, drained and flaked	8 oz
50g/2 oz	black (ripe) olives	⅓ cup
4 × 15ml spoons/ 4 tablespoons	sauce vinaigrette (page 78)	5 tablespoons
	salt, freshly ground pepper	
	GARNISH anchovy fillets, drained	

Line a large salad bowl with the lettuce leaves. Put the beans, eggs, tomatoes, garlic, tuna, most of the olives and the sauce into a bowl, and toss lightly. Season to taste, then pile into the centre of the salad bowl, and garnish with the remaining olives and the anchovy fillets before serving.

Escargots de Bourgogne

(Snails in Garlic Butter)

Metric/imperial		American
	24 canned snails	
4 × 15ml spoons/ 4 tablespoons	shallots, finely chopped	5 tablespoons
	4 cloves garlic, finely chopped	
4 × 15ml spoons/ 4 tablespoons	dry white wine	5 tablespoons
225g/8 oz	butter	1 cup
3–4 × 15ml spoons/ 3–4 tablespoons	fresh parsley, chopped	4–5 tablespoons
	juice of ½ lemon	
	salt, freshly ground pepper	
2 × 15ml spoons/ 2 tablespoons	pastis	3 tablespoons

Open the snails and drain in a nylon sieve or strainer. Simmer the shallots and garlic in the wine until the liquid has evaporated. Beat the wine mixture into the butter with the parsley, lemon juice, seasoning and pastis. Put one snail in each snail shell, and cover thickly with flavoured butter. Put the shells, open side up, in a snail plate or on a bed of coarse salt, and heat in a fairly hot oven, 200°C/400°F Gas 6, for 5–6 minutes until the butter is melted and very hot. Serve at once.

Huîtres

(Oysters)

6–12 oysters	
½ lemon	

Carefully scrub the oysters under cold running water, discarding any which are open. Just before serving, open (shuck) the oysters and remove the 'beards'. Leave each oyster in its shell. Serve on a bed of ice cubes with half a lemon.

Mousse au Saumon

(Salmon Mousse)

SERVES 6–8

Metric/imperial		American
450g/1 lb	cut of salmon	1 lb
1.2 litres/2 pints	court bouillon (page 79)	5 cups
300ml/½ pint	Sauce Béchamel (page 75)	1¼ cups
50g/2 oz	butter	¼ cup
10 × 5ml spoons/ 10 teaspoons	double (heavy) cream	10 teaspoons
1 × 15ml spoon/ 1 tablespoon	medium-dry sherry	1 tablespoon
	GARNISH cucumber slices	
	sprigs watercress	

Put the salmon in a large pan and cover with the *court bouillon*. Heat to boiling point, then simmer for 15 minutes. Drain, cool, remove the skin and bones, then pound or process in a blender or food processor until smooth.

Put the cold *Sauce Béchamel* into a bowl, add the salmon, and mix until completely blended. Cream the butter until soft, whip the cream until semi-stiff, and add to the mixture together with the sherry. Stir well, then put the mousse into an oiled ring mould. Smooth the top, and leave to set in a refrigerator.

Before serving, dip the base of the mould into warm water, and turn the mousse out on to a large platter. Garnish with cucumber slices and watercress.

Serve with sliced brown bread and butter.

Mousse au Saumon

Tartelettes de Foie de Volaille

Tartelettes de Foie de Volaille

(Chicken Liver Tartlets)

Metric/imperial		American
350g/12 oz	prepared shortcrust (pie) pastry	¾ lb
450g/1 lb	small turnips, peeled and sliced	1 lb
	salt, freshly ground pepper	
	chicken stock	
	ground nutmeg	
	1 egg yolk	
3 × 15ml spoons/ 3 tablespoons	double (heavy) cream	4 tablespoons
40g/1½ oz	butter	3 tablespoons
	8 chicken livers, sliced	
2 × 15ml spoons/ 2 tablespoons	dry sherry	3 tablespoons
75g/3 oz	button mushrooms, thinly sliced	¾ cup
4 × 15ml spoons/ 4 tablespoons	consommé (page 10)	5 tablespoons
	GARNISH	
	young spinach leaves	
	sprigs watercress	

Roll out the pastry on a lightly floured surface, and cut out four pastry cases (pie shells) using a 10cm/4 inch fluted pastry cutter. Bake blind in a fairly hot oven, 200°C/400°F/ Gas 6, for 20–30 minutes.

Meanwhile, put the turnips into a pan with salt and pepper to taste, the chicken stock and a generous pinch of nutmeg. Heat slowly to boiling point, then simmer until the turnips are just tender. Drain thoroughly, then mash with the egg yolk and cream. Keep warm.

Melt the butter in a pan, and fry the livers until sealed on the outside but still pink in the centre. Add the sherry, mushrooms and seasoning to taste, then simmer steadily for a further 3 minutes. Stir in the consommé, and bubble briskly for 1 minute. Keep warm.

Fill the warm pastry cases (pie shells) with the purée, and top with the chicken liver mixture. Arrange on a large serving platter, and garnish with spinach leaves and watercress.

Tarte à L'Oignon Alsacienne

(Alsace Onion Tart)

SERVES 4–6

Metric/imperial		American
300g/11 oz	prepared shortcrust (pie) pastry	scant ¾ lb
50g/2 oz	butter	¼ cup
675g/1½ lb	onions, thinly sliced	1½ lb
	2 eggs	
10 × 5ml spoons/ 10 teaspoons	milk	10 teaspoons
150ml/¼ pint	single (light) cream	⅔ cup
	salt, freshly ground pepper	
	a pinch of ground nutmeg	

Roll out the pastry on a lightly floured surface and use to line a 20cm/8 inch flan (pie) ring placed on a baking sheet. Bake blind in a fairly hot oven, 200°C/400°F/Gas 6, for 10 minutes.

Melt the butter in a pan, and cook the onions for about 20–30 minutes until soft. Beat together the eggs, milk, cream, salt, pepper and nutmeg until fully mixed, then pour a layer into the pastry case (pie shell). Cover with the onions, then pour in the remaining custard mixture. Bake in a fairly hot oven, 200°C/400°F/Gas 6, for 30 minutes until the tart is golden-brown.

Tarte à L'Oignon Alsacienne

Quiche aux Poireaux

(Leek Tart)

SERVES 8

Metric/imperial		American
	8 small leeks, white parts only	
250g/9 oz	prepared shortcrust (pie) pastry	generous $\frac{1}{2}$ lb
	2 eggs	
150ml/$\frac{1}{4}$ pint	Sauce Béchamel (page 75)	$\frac{2}{3}$ cup
	salt, freshly ground pepper	
25g/1 oz	Gruyère cheese, grated	$\frac{1}{4}$ cup

Tie the leeks into two bundles with string. Heat a pan of salted water to boiling point, put in the leeks, and cook at a gentle boil for 10 minutes. Drain, then squeeze as dry as possible. Slice the leeks thickly.

Roll out the pastry 6mm/$\frac{1}{4}$ inch thick on a lightly floured surface, and use to line a 17.5cm/7 inch flan (pie) ring placed on a baking sheet. Bake blind in a fairly hot oven, 200°C/400°F/Gas 6, for 15 minutes, then remove the paper and dry filling, and bake for a further 5 minutes. Leave to cool.

Beat together the eggs and sauce, and season to taste. Add half the cheese, blending it in well. Put a layer of flavoured sauce in the cooled pastry case (pie shell), cover with the leeks, then with the remaining sauce. Sprinkle with the remaining cheese, and bake in a fairly hot oven, 190°C/375°F/Gas 5, for 20 minutes or until golden on top.

Quiche Lorraine

SERVES 4–6

Metric/imperial		American
250g/9 oz	prepared shortcrust (pie) pastry	generous $\frac{1}{2}$ lb
	6 rashers (slices) streaky bacon, without rinds and cut into pieces	
	3 eggs	
300ml/$\frac{1}{2}$ pint	single (light) cream	$1\frac{1}{4}$ cups
	salt, freshly ground pepper	
	a pinch of ground nutmeg	
25g/1 oz	butter	2 tablespoons

Roll out the pastry on a lightly floured surface and use to line a 17.5cm/7 inch flan (pie) ring placed on a baking sheet. Bake blind in a fairly hot oven, 200°C/400°F/Gas 6, for 10 minutes until the rim of the pastry is slightly browned but the base is still soft.

Blanch the bacon in boiling water for 3 minutes, then drain well and scatter the pieces over the pastry case (pie shell). Press in lightly. Beat together the eggs, cream, seasoning and nutmeg until fully mixed, then pour the mixture into the pastry case (pie shell). Dot with flakes of butter. Bake in a fairly hot oven, 190°C/375°F/Gas 5, for 30 minutes. Serve at once.

Quiche Lorraine

FISH AND SHELLFISH

Sole Véronique

Metric/imperial		American
	4 large lemon sole or flounder fillets, skinned	
	2 shallots, chopped	
50g/2 oz	button mushrooms, chopped	$\frac{1}{2}$ cup
	sprigs parsley	
	1 bay leaf	
	salt, freshly ground pepper	
150ml/$\frac{1}{4}$ pint	dry white wine	$\frac{2}{3}$ cup
150ml/$\frac{1}{4}$ pint	water	$\frac{2}{3}$ cup
25g/1 oz	butter	2 tablespoons
2 × 15ml spoons/ 2 tablespoons	flour	3 tablespoons
150ml/$\frac{1}{4}$ pint	milk	$\frac{2}{3}$ cup
100g/4 oz	small white (green) grapes, skinned and pips removed	$\frac{1}{4}$ lb
	juice of $\frac{1}{2}$ lemon	
2 × 15ml spoons/ 2 tablespoons	single (light) cream	3 tablespoons
	GARNISH	
	fleurons (page 79)	
	chopped parsley	

Lay the fillets in a shallow ovenproof dish, and sprinkle with the shallots and mushrooms. Add the herbs, season well, and pour the wine and water over the fish. Cover and cook in a fairly hot oven, 190°C/375°F/Gas 5, for 15 minutes.

Drain the fish, and keep it hot. Reserve the cooking liquid, and reduce it to half by boiling uncovered. Melt the butter in a pan and stir in the flour. Cook for 2–3 minutes without colouring, then add the cooking liquid and milk gradually, stirring all the time, and heat the sauce until it thickens. Stir in the grapes, saving a few to garnish the dish. Add the lemon juice and cream. Pour the sauce over the fish, and garnish with the reserved grapes, the *fleurons* and chopped parsley. Serve at once.

Sole Bonne Femme

Metric/imperial		American
75g/3 oz	butter	6 tablespoons
	4 shallots, chopped	
100g/4 oz	mushrooms, sliced	1 cup
2 × 15ml spoons/ 2 tablespoons	fresh parsley, chopped	3 tablespoons
4 × 225g/8 oz	sole or flounder fillets, cut in half lengthways and skinned	4 × $\frac{1}{2}$ lb
	salt, freshly ground pepper	
4 × 15ml spoons/ 4 tablespoons	dry white wine	5 tablespoons
150ml/$\frac{1}{4}$ pint	chicken stock	$\frac{2}{3}$ cup
2 × 15ml spoons/ 2 tablespoons	lemon juice	3 tablespoons
25g/1 oz	flour	$\frac{1}{4}$ cup
	GARNISH	
	chopped parsley	
	halved mushrooms	
	lemon twists	

Melt 50g/2 oz/$\frac{1}{4}$ US cup butter in a pan, and fry the shallots and mushrooms until soft. Add the parsley, then spread in the base of an ovenproof dish. Roll up the sole fillets from head to tail, put into the dish, and season well. Pour over the wine, stock and lemon juice, and cook in a moderate oven, 180°C/350°F/Gas 4, for 15 minutes.

Meanwhile, knead together the remaining butter with the flour to form a paste. Transfer the sole to a heated serving dish, and keep hot. Add the beurre manié, off heat, in small pieces to the cooking liquor, stirring until dissolved. Heat until the sauce thickens, then pour this over the fish. Serve hot, garnished with parsley, mushrooms and lemon twists.

Sole Bonne Femme

Filets de Sole au Melon à la Menthe

(Fillets of Sole with Mint Sauce and Melon)

Metric/imperial		American
	8 sole or flounder fillets, skinned	
	salt, freshly ground pepper	
2 × 15ml spoons/ 2 tablespoons	fresh mint, chopped	3 tablespoons
300ml/½ pint	dry white wine	1¼ cups
	1 Ogen or Charentais (Cantaloupe or Crenshaw) melon, halved and de-seeded	
150ml/¼ pint	double (heavy) cream	⅔ cup
	sprigs mint	

Sprinkle the sole with salt and pepper to taste and with half the chopped mint. Roll up each fillet, and place in a deep frying pan (skillet). Sprinkle with the remaining chopped mint, then add the wine. Cover, then poach gently for about 12 minutes until the fish is just tender.

Meanwhile, scoop the melon flesh into balls, then scoop out any remaining melon flesh attached to the skin (this is added to the sauce).

Transfer the cooked sole fillets to a warmed serving dish, and keep hot. Boil the cooking liquid until reduced, together with the remnants of melon flesh, and whisk until smooth. Stir in the cream, and heat the sauce through. Spoon the hot sauce evenly over the fish, and garnish with the prepared melon balls and the sprigs of mint.

Filets de Sole au Melon à la Menthe

Sole Colbert

Metric/imperial		American
	6 Dover soles or flounders, skinned	
100g/4 oz	flour	1 cup
	salt, freshly ground pepper	
	2 eggs, beaten	
	fresh white breadcrumbs	
	fat for deep frying	
	COLBERT BUTTER 8–16 large sprigs parsley, blanched and finely chopped	
225g/8 oz	butter, softened	1 cup
	salt, freshly ground pepper	
	lemon juice	
2 × 5ml spoons/ 2 teaspoons	tarragon, finely chopped	2 teaspoons
2 × 15ml spoons/ 2 tablespoons	meat jelly, dissolved	3 tablespoons
	GARNISH sprigs parsley	
	lemon wedges	

Cut down the backbone of the fish on the skinned side, and slice under the flesh, following the bones to make a pocket on each side. Cut the backbone in three places with sharp scissors, to allow removal after cooking.

Season the flour with salt and pepper. Coat the fish with the flour, then with egg and breadcrumbs. Deep fry until golden-brown, then drain. Remove the bone where cut, and arrange the fish on a serving dish. Keep hot.

To make the Colbert Butter, work the parsley into the butter with the seasonings and lemon juice, then mix together with the chopped tarragon and meat jelly.

Fill the pockets of the fish with the Colbert butter, and serve at once, garnished with sprigs of parsley and lemon wedges.

Raie au Beurre Noir

(Skate in Black Butter)

SERVES 3–4

Metric/imperial		American
	1–2 skate wings, cut into serving portions	
1.2 litres/2 pints	court bouillon (page 79)	5 cups
	BLACK BUTTER	
25g/1 oz	butter	2 tablespoons
	salt, freshly ground black pepper	
2 × 15ml spoons/ 2 tablespoons	capers	3 tablespoons
4 × 5ml spoons/ 4 teaspoons	fresh parsley, chopped	4 teaspoons
5 × 15ml spoons/ 5 tablespoons	wine vinegar	6 tablespoons

Put the fish in a deep frying pan (skillet) and cover with the *court bouillon*. Heat to boiling point, then simmer for 15–20 minutes. Lift out the fish, drain, and gently scrape away the skin. Place in an ovenproof dish and keep hot.

To make the black butter, pour off the stock, put in the butter, and heat until it is a rich golden-brown colour. Spoon it quickly over the fish, season with salt and pepper, and scatter the capers and chopped parsley over the fish. Add the vinegar to the pan, heat quickly, and pour over the fish. Serve at once.

Raie au Beurre Noir

Roujet en Papillote

Roujet en Papillote

(Red Mullet Baked in Foil)

SERVES 6

Metric/imperial		American
	6 red mullet	
50g/2 oz	butter	¼ cup
	salt, freshly ground pepper	
	juice of ½ lemon	
	GARNISH lemon wedges	
	sprigs parsley	

Lay each mullet on a piece of foil large enough to enclose it completely. Dot with butter, sprinkle with salt and pepper, and add a little lemon juice. Fasten the packages by pressing the edges of the foil firmly together over the fish. Cook in a fairly hot oven, 190°C/375°F/Gas 5, for 20–30 minutes.

Remove the fish from the foil and place on a warmed plate. Pour the liquid from the foil packages over the fish, and garnish with lemon wedges and sprigs of parsley.

Truite aux Amandes

(Trout with Almonds)

Metric/imperial		American
100g/4 oz	butter	½ cup
	4 trout	
	salt, freshly ground pepper	
	juice of ½ lemon	
50g/2 oz	flaked blanched (slivered) almonds	½ cup
150ml/¼ pint	double (heavy) cream	⅔ cup
	3 egg yolks	
	GARNISH sprigs parsley	

Melt the butter in a grill (broiler) pan under medium heat. Lay the trout in the pan, season, and sprinkle with lemon juice. Grill (broil) for 5 minutes, then turn the fish. Sprinkle with most of the almonds, spread the rest at the side of the pan, and continue grilling (broiling) for a further 3–5 minutes until the trout are tender and the almonds are browned. Drain, then put the almonds to one side.

Mix the cream with the yolks, and put into a small pan with any juices from the pan. Heat gently, stirring well, until thickened; do not let the mixture boil.

Lay the trout on a serving dish, and spoon the cream sauce over them. Garnish with the reserved almonds and with sprigs of parsley.

Quenelles de Brochet

(Pike Dumplings)

SERVES 4–6

Metric/imperial		American
450g/1 lb	pike fillets, skinned and diced	1 lb
	4–5 egg whites	
600ml/1 pint	double (heavy) cream	2½ cups
	salt, freshly ground pepper	
	a pinch of ground nutmeg	
1.2 litres/2 pints	court bouillon (page 79)	5 cups

Mix together the fish and egg whites, and process in a blender or food processor, then rub the mixture through a sieve. Whip the cream to the same consistency as the fish purée, and fold it in lightly but thoroughly. Season the mixture with salt, pepper and nutmeg, then chill in a refrigerator for several hours.

Heat the *court bouillon* until just simmering. Shape the chilled fish mixture into quenelles with warmed rounded dessertspoons, and gently lower into the liquid. Simmer for 8–10 minutes, then drain with a perforated spoon. Serve at once.

Goujons de Carrelet

(Deep-fried Strips of Plaice)

SERVES 6

Metric/imperial		American
	flour for coating	
	salt, freshly ground pepper	
	12 plaice (flounder) fillets, cut length-ways into short strips (2.5–5cm/1–2 inches wide)	
100ml/4 fl oz	milk	½ cup
	oil for deep frying	
	GARNISH	
	sprigs parsley	
	lemon wedges	

Season the flour with salt and pepper. Dip the fish in the milk, then coat with the flour, shaking off any excess. Deep fry until golden-brown, then arrange on a dish and serve hot, garnished with the parsley and lemon wedges.

Serve with *Sauce Tartare* (page 78).

Turbot Dugléré

(Turbot with Tomatoes and Onions)

Metric/imperial		American
5 × 5ml spoons/ 5 teaspoons	cooking oil	5 teaspoons
25g/1 oz	butter	2 tablespoons
25g/1 oz	onions, chopped	¼ cup
225g/8 oz	tomatoes, chopped	½ lb
5 × 5ml spoons/ 5 teaspoons	white wine vinegar	5 teaspoons
200ml/⅓ pint	dry white wine	⅞ cup
1.35kg/3 lb	turbot or halibut, skinned and filletted (trimmings reserved)	3 lb
	salt, freshly ground pepper	
	bouquet garni	
2 × 5ml spoons/ 2 teaspoons	softened butter	2 teaspoons
4 × 5ml spoons/ 4 teaspoons	flour	4 teaspoons
	GARNISH	
	chopped parsley	
	chopped tarragon	
	juice of ½ lemon	

Heat the oil and butter in a sauté pan, and cook the onions for 2–3 minutes, without colouring, until soft. Add the tomatoes, vinegar and wine. Simmer for 10 minutes, then leave to cool.

Place the fish in a greased shallow ovenproof dish, season to taste, and cover with the wine mixture. Cover and cook in a fairly hot oven, 190°C/375°F/Gas 5, for 20 minutes.

Boil the fish trimmings in 300ml/½ pint/1¼ US cups water with the bouquet garni for 15 minutes, then strain the liquid into a small saucepan. Knead together the butter and flour to a smooth paste, and add this, off heat, in small pieces to the fish stock, stirring until dissolved. Heat until the sauce thickens. Season to taste, then pour this over the fish. Sprinkle with parsley and tarragon and a squeeze of lemon just before serving.

Tranche de Thon à la Concombre

(Tuna and Cucumber in Puff Pastry)

SERVES 4–6

Metric/imperial		American
350g/12 oz	prepared puff pastry	¾ lb
	1 egg, beaten	
25g/1 oz	butter	2 tablespoons
400g/14 oz	canned tuna, flaked into large pieces	14 oz
	1 medium onion, finely chopped	
350g/12 oz	cucumber, peeled, de-seeded and cubed	2 cups
1 × 15ml spoon/ 1 tablespoon	flour	1 tablespoon
150ml/¼ pint	water	⅔ cup
	1 chicken stock (bouillon) cube	
2 × 15ml spoons/ 2 tablespoons	double (heavy) cream	3 tablespoons
	grated rind and juice of ½ lemon	
	salt, freshly ground pepper	
	GARNISH chopped parsley	
	strips of lemon rind	

Roll out the pastry on a lightly floured surface to a rectangle 25 × 15cm/10 × 6 inches. Cut a 2.5cm/1 inch border, and remove the inner rectangle. Roll this back to the original size, then place on a wetted baking sheet, brush the outside edge with water, and carefully place the pastry border on top. Press down gently, then mark a pattern around the border with the back of a knife. Prick the centre of the pastry with a fork, then glaze the pastry border with a little of the beaten egg. Bake in a fairly hot oven, 200°C/400°F/ Gas 6, for 20–25 minutes until crisp and golden.

Meanwhile, heat the butter and the oil from the tuna fish in a saucepan, and cook the onion until transparent. Add the cucumber, and cook for 5 minutes, then stir in the flour, water and stock (bouillon) cube. Heat to boiling point, stirring all the time, then reduce the heat, add the tuna fish, and simmer until the sauce thickens. Stir the cream, lemon rind and juice into the remaining beaten egg, then, off the heat, stir the lemon mixture into the tuna sauce. Stir carefully over gentle heat until thickened. Do not allow the sauce to boil. Season to taste.

Place the pastry case on a serving plate, spoon the tuna filling into the centre, and garnish with chopped parsley and strips of lemon rind.

Maquereau Niçoise

(Mackerel in Tomato Sauce)

Metric/imperial		American
2 × 15ml spoons/ 2 tablespoons	olive oil	3 tablespoons
25g/1 oz	butter	2 tablespoons
	1 large onion, finely chopped	
	1 clove of garlic, crushed	
	4 small mackerel, cleaned	
150ml/¼ pint	medium-dry white wine	⅔ cup
2 × 5ml spoons/ 2 teaspoons	concentrated tomato purée (paste)	2 teaspoons
	a pinch of powdered saffron	
	salt, freshly ground pepper	
225g/8 oz	tomatoes, skinned and chopped	1 cup
	GARNISH sprigs parsley	
	stoned (pitted) olives	
	lemon slices	

Heat together the oil and butter in a large frying pan (skillet), and cook the onion and garlic until soft, then place the fish on top. Pour the wine and tomato purée (paste) over the fish, and season with the saffron, salt and pepper. Poach gently for 10 minutes, then transfer to a plate, and keep warm.

Add the tomatoes to the sauce, and boil briskly for 5 minutes, then pour it over the fish. Garnish with parsley, olives and lemon slices.

Tranche de Thon à la Concombre

Coquilles St Jacques Mornay

(Scallops Mornay)

Metric/imperial		American
450g/1 lb	scallops	1 lb
	1 small onion, sliced	
	salt, freshly ground pepper	
	1 bay leaf	
10 × 5ml spoons/ 10 teaspoons	dry white wine	10 teaspoons
5 × 15ml spoons/ 5 tablespoons	water	6 tablespoons
	juice of ½ lemon	
25g/1 oz	butter	2 tablespoons
25g/1 oz	flour	¼ cup
150ml/¼ pint	milk	⅔ cup
5 × 15ml spoons/ 5 tablespoons	single (light) cream	6 tablespoons
225g/8 oz	mashed potato	1 cup
3 × 15ml spoons/ 3 tablespoons	dry white breadcrumbs	4 tablespoons
4 × 15ml spoons/ 4 tablespoons	Parmesan cheese, grated	5 tablespoons

Place the scallops in a pan with the onion, seasoning and bay leaf. Pour the wine, water and lemon juice over them, and poach gently for 5 minutes. Strain off the liquid, and put to one side with the scallops.

Melt the butter in a pan, then stir in the flour. Blend in the liquid strained from the scallops, and stir over gentle heat until the sauce starts to thicken. Add the milk, and simmer for 2–3 minutes, then stir in the cream.

Slice the scallops, then divide between four lightly greased scallop shells or suitable flameproof dishes. Coat with the sauce, then pipe the mashed potato around the edges of each shell. Sprinkle lightly with the breadcrumbs and Parmesan cheese, and cook in a fairly hot oven, 200°C/400°F/Gas 6, for 10–15 minutes.

Langoustine Provençale

(Scampi in Tomato and Mushroom Sauce)

Metric/imperial		American
	2 shallots, finely chopped	
	bouquet garni	
150ml/¼ pint	dry white wine	⅔ cup
50g/2 oz	butter	¼ cup
2 × 15ml spoons/ 2 tablespoons	flour	3 tablespoons
	1 clove of garlic, chopped	
2 × 5ml spoons/ 2 teaspoons	concentrated tomato purée (paste)	2 teaspoons
300ml/½ pint	stock	1¼ cups
	flour for coating	
	salt, freshly ground pepper	
450g/1 lb	peeled scampi (shelled jumbo shrimp)	1 lb
75g/3 oz	button mushrooms, sliced	¾ cup
	3 tomatoes, sliced	
	GARNISH chopped parsley	

Put the shallots in a saucepan with the bouquet garni and the wine. Boil, uncovered, until the liquid is reduced by half, then put to one side.

Melt 1 × 15ml spoon/1 tablespoon of the butter in another saucepan, add the flour, and cook for 2–3 minutes, stirring all the time. Add the garlic with the tomato purée (paste) and stock. Simmer for 10–15 minutes, then pour in the wine, and cook for a further 5 minutes. Add the remaining butter, and keep warm.

Season the flour with salt and pepper. Roll the scampi (shrimp) in the seasoned flour, and shallow fry gently in 25g/1 oz/2 US tablespoons butter for 3–5 minutes. Remove with a perforated spoon, place on a serving dish, and keep warm.

Sauté the mushrooms and tomatoes in the fat left in the pan, then add them to the sauce. Boil for 2 minutes, then spoon the sauce over the scampi (shrimp). Sprinkle with chopped parsley.

Serve with boiled rice.

Moules à la Marinière

Moules à la Marinière

(Mussels with White Wine)

SERVES 4–6

Metric/imperial		American
1.35kg/3 lb	live mussels	3 lb
	1 onion, sliced	
	1 carrot, sliced	
	1 stick of celery, sliced	
	bouquet garni	
150ml/¼ pint	water	⅔ cup
150ml/¼ pint	white wine	⅔ cup
25g/1 oz	butter	2 tablespoons
1 × 15ml spoon/ 1 tablespoon	flour	1 tablespoon
	pepper	
	GARNISH chopped parsley	

Scrub and beard the mussels, making sure that all are tightly closed, then put them into a large pan. Tuck the vegetables among them with the bouquet garni. Pour over the water and wine, and place over moderate heat. Leave until the liquid boils up over the mussels. Shake the pan a few times, then put to one side.

Strain the liquid from the pan of mussels, through muslin (cheesecloth), into a smaller pan, and keep the mussels warm. Knead together the butter and flour to a smooth paste, and add this, off heat, to the liquid in small pieces, stirring until dissolved. Heat until boiling, then season well with pepper.

Put the mussels into a deep dish, and pour over the cooking liquid. Sprinkle with chopped parsley.

Serve with pieces of crusty bread.

MEAT AND POULTRY

Steak au Poivre

Metric/imperial		American
	4 fillet (filet mignon), sirloin or entrecôte steaks (175g/6 oz each)	
	1 clove of garlic, cut in half	
4 × 15ml spoons/ 4 tablespoons	olive oil	5 tablespoons
4 × 15ml spoons/ 4 tablespoons	whole black and white peppercorns, coarsely crushed in a mortar	5 tablespoons
50g/2 oz	unsalted butter	¼ cup
	GARNISH Beurre à la Maître d'Hotel (page 79)	

Rub the steaks on both sides with the garlic, and brush each side with the olive oil. With the heel of your hand, press the crushed peppercorns into the surface of the meat on each side.

Melt the butter in a frying pan (skillet), and fry the steaks over high heat for 1 minute on both sides until sealed and browned. Reduce the heat and fry the steaks for 4–5 minutes for rare, 7 minutes for medium-rare, and 9 minutes for well-done steaks, turning them a few times. Place on a warmed serving dish, and garnish with pats of *Beurre à la Maître d'Hotel* . Serve at once.

Steak Diane

Metric/imperial		American
75g/3 oz	unsalted butter	6 tablespoons
	1 small onion	
	4 minute, fillet (filet mignon) or rump steaks (175g/6 oz each), beaten flat to 6mm/ ¼ inch thickness	
	grated rind and juice of 1 lemon	
1 × 5ml spoon/ 1 teaspoon	caster sugar	1 teaspoon
	Worcestershire sauce	
1 × 15ml spoon/ 1 tablespoon	fresh parsley, chopped	1 tablespoon
2 × 15ml spoons/ 2 tablespoons	brandy	3 tablespoons

Melt 50g/2 oz/¼ US cup of the butter in a large, heavy-based frying pan (skillet) and fry the onion for about 5 minutes until soft. Remove from the pan and keep warm on a plate.

Raise the heat under the pan. Using the remaining butter, fry two steaks at a time over high heat for 1 minute on each side. Remove from the pan and keep warm.

Return the onion to the pan, and add the lemon rind and juice, the sugar, and a few drops of Worcestershire sauce. Stir in the parsley, and cook lightly. Warm the brandy separately.

Put the steaks into the pan, and flame with the warmed brandy. Serve at once, with the sauce spooned over them, and accompanied by chipped potatoes (French fries), grilled (broiled) mushrooms and tomatoes.

Chateaubriand

(Grilled Double Fillet Steak)

SERVES 2

a double fillet steak (filet mignon), not less than 5cm/2 inches thick
olive oil
freshly ground pepper
GARNISH Beurre à la Maître d'Hôtel (page 79)

Brush both sides of the steak with oil, and season with pepper. Place on a greased grid, and cook under a very hot grill (broiler) until browned and sealed. Turn the steak over, and grill (broil) until browned. Reduce the heat slightly and continue cooking for 4–5 minutes, turning it once or twice, until the steak is well browned on the outside but slightly underdone on the inside. Garnish with pats of *Beurre à la Maître d'Hôtel* , and serve at once.

Note To serve, slice downwards at a slight angle into four to six even slices.

Tournedos Rossini

Tournedos Rossini

(Tournedos with Pâté and Mushrooms)

Metric/imperial		American
	4 slices white bread	
100g/4 oz	butter	½ cup
1 × 15ml spoon/ 1 tablespoon	cooking oil	1 tablespoon
	4 tournedos steaks (175g/6 oz each approx)	
10 × 5ml spoons/ 10 teaspoons	Madeira	10 teaspoons
5 × 15ml spoons/ 5 tablespoons	beef stock	6 tablespoons
100ml/4 fl oz	Sauce Espagnole (page 75)	½ cup
	salt, freshly ground pepper	
	4 rounds good quality liver pâté (6mm/¼ inch thick)	
	4 small flat mushrooms	
4 × 5ml spoons/ 4 teaspoons	chilled butter	4 teaspoons
	sprigs watercress	

Cut four rounds from the bread slices, a little wider than the bases of the steaks. Heat 50g/2 oz/¼ US cup butter and the oil in a large, deep frying pan (skillet), and fry the bread rounds over moderate heat until light golden and crisp on both sides. Transfer to a warmed serving dish and keep warm.

Put 25g/1 oz/2 US tablespoons butter into the pan. Pat the tournedos dry, add to the pan, raise the heat, and fry the steaks quickly, turning as required, until they are well seared and browned all over but rare inside. Place them on the fried bread rounds, and keep warm.

Lower the heat and stir the wine and stock quickly into the pan. Simmer for 3 minutes, then stir in the sauce, season to taste, and simmer until reduced to the desired consistency.

Meanwhile, melt the remaining butter in a small frying pan (skillet), and turn the pâté slices and mushrooms in it for 2–3 minutes over high heat, until the mushrooms are soft and the pâté is lightly browned but not melted.

Place a slice of pâté on each tournedos, and cap it with a mushroom, gill side down. Garnish the top of each mushroom with 1 × 5ml spoon/1 teaspoon chilled butter. Serve at once, with the sauce in a warmed sauce-boat. Garnish the dish with watercress, and offer a peppermill of black pepper with the steaks.

Boeuf à la Bourguignonne

Boeuf à la Bourguignonne

(Beef Bourguignonne)

SERVES 4–6

Metric/imperial		American
550g/1¼ lb	chuck steak, cut into 2.5cm/1 inch cubes	1¼ lb
300ml/½ pint	red wine	1¼ cups
½ × 2.5ml spoon/ ¼ teaspoon	black pepper	¼ teaspoon
1 × 2.5ml spoon ½ teaspoon	salt	½ teaspoon
	bouquet garni	
	1 small onion, finely sliced	
	1 small carrot, finely sliced	
	2 cloves garlic, crushed	
3 × 15ml spoons/ 3 tablespoons	oil	4 tablespoons
	2 rashers (slices) bacon, without rinds and cut into small pieces	
	12 button (pickling) onions	
	12 button mushrooms	
25g/1oz	flour	¼ cup
	salt, freshly ground pepper	
300ml/½ pint (approx)	beef stock	1¼ cups (approx)
GARNISH		
	sippets of fried bread	
	chopped parsley	

Put the steak in a basin, pour the wine over it, and add the pepper, salt and bouquet garni. Add the onion, carrot and garlic, cover and leave to marinate for about 6 hours.

Heat most of the oil in a frying pan (skillet), add the bacon, and fry lightly, then remove and put to one side. Fry the onions and the mushrooms in the oil for 3–4 minutes, then remove and put to one side.

Drain the meat, reserving the marinade, and pat dry on soft kitchen paper. Season the flour with salt and pepper, and coat the meat in the flour. Add a little more oil to the pan and fry the meat until sealed all over. Put into an ovenproof casserole, then stir in the bacon, onions and mushrooms. Strain the marinade over the meat and add the stock. Cover and cook in a warm oven, 160°C/325°F/Gas 3, for about 2 hours. Season to taste. Serve garnished with sippets and chopped parsley.

Bifteck à L'Américaine

(Steak Tartare)

Metric/imperial		American
450g/1lb	lean fillet (tender-loin), rump steak or topside (top round of beef), finely minced	1 lb
	salt, freshly ground black pepper	
	6 shallots, chopped	
6 × 15ml spoons/ 6 tablespoons	chopped capers	7 tablespoons
3 × 15ml spoons/ 3 tablespoons	fresh parsley, chopped	4 tablespoons
	4 egg yolks (in half shells)	
GARNISH		
	8 anchovy fillets, drained	
	paprika	

Season the meat well, then form into four thick patties; put each on a separate plate. Arrange small mounds of the chopped shallots, capers and parsley around the meat. Make a hollow in the centre of each patty, and put in it the egg yolk, still in the half shell. Alternatively, cross two anchovy fillets over each yolk if not using the shells. Sprinkle with paprika.

Provide oil and vinegar separately. At the table, the ingredients are mixed together with a fork.

Boeuf à la Mode

(Marinated Beef Casserole)

SERVES 8

Metric/imperial		American
25g/1 oz	butter	2 tablespoons
900g/2 lb	rump of beef	2 lb
	10 button (pickling) onions	
25g/1 oz	flour	¼ cup
900ml/1½ pints	beef stock	3¾ cups
	salt, freshly ground pepper	
	2 rashers (slices) streaky bacon, without rinds	
	2 medium carrots, thinly sliced	
	MARINADE	
	1 small onion, finely chopped	
100ml/4 fl oz	claret	½ cup
	juice of ½ lemon	
	2 cloves	
	salt, freshly ground pepper	
	bouquet garni	

Make the marinade first. Mix together all the ingredients, put in the meat, and leave for 2 hours, basting frequently. Drain the beef thoroughly, then strain and reserve the marinade.

Melt the butter in a large pan and fry the meat, turning it until browned on all sides. Fry the button (pickling) onions at the same time, turning them so that they brown evenly. Remove the beef and onions, and put to one side. Stir the flour into the fat in the pan, and cook until browned. Gradually add the stock and the marinade, and stir until boiling. Replace the meat and onions, then season to taste. Cover the top of the meat with the bacon, then add the carrots. Transfer to an ovenproof dish, cover and cook in a warm oven, 160°C/325°F/Gas 3, for 2 hours. When tender, transfer to a warmed serving dish, and keep hot. Strain the liquid remaining in the casserole, and pour it over the meat.

Pot-au-Feu

SERVES 6

Metric/imperial		American
900g/2 lb	brisket of beef	2 lb
225g/8 oz	shin (shank) of beef, chopped	½ lb
2 × 5ml spoons/ 2 teaspoons	salt	2 teaspoons
	6 black peppercorns	
2.4 litres/4 pints	water	5 pints
	bouquet garni	
	4 cloves	
	4 medium onions	
	4 medium carrots, cut into large pieces	
	2 small turnips, cut into large pieces	
	1 small parsnip, cut into large pieces	
	2 leeks, cut into large pieces	
	¼ small cabbage, shredded	
	2 tomatoes, skinned and chopped	
450g/1 lb	medium potatoes, peeled	1 lb
	salt, freshly ground pepper	
	6 slices French bread	

Put the meats into a large pan, add the salt, peppercorns and water, and soak for 30 minutes. Heat slowly to boiling point, add the bouquet garni, then simmer gently for 1 hour, skimming the surface occasionally.

Press a clove into each onion. Add the carrots, turnips, parsnip and leeks to the broth with the whole onions. Bring back to simmering point, half cover, and simmer gently for a further 2¼ hours, skimming from time to time. Add the cabbage, tomatoes and potatoes, bring back to simmering point, and simmer for a further 30 minutes.

Serve the meat with the potatoes and some of the large pieces of vegetable around it; keep this covered and hot.

Discard any bones and the bouquet garni from the broth. Measure 1.2 litres/2 pints/5 US cups of the broth into a clean pan. Cut 6mm/¼ inch cubes from the carrot, leek, parsnip and turnip, put 1 × 15ml spoon/1 tablespoon of each into the broth, re-heat it, then season to taste. Toast the slices of French bread until golden, and float them in the broth. Serve as a first course, followed by the meat and vegetables.

Alouettes sans Têtes

(Beef Olives)

SERVES 8

Metric/imperial		American
	18 slices topside (top round) of beef (25g/1 oz each)	
	French (Dijon-style) mustard	
	salt, freshly ground pepper	
	STUFFING	
50g/2 oz	butter	¼ cup
	1 shallot, chopped	
	1 large clove of garlic, chopped	
100g/4 oz	green (Canadian) bacon, without rinds and chopped	¼ lb
175g/6 oz	cooked chicken, chopped	¾ cup
75g/3 oz	fresh breadcrumbs	1½ cups
2 × 15ml spoons/ 2 tablespoons	brandy	3 tablespoons
	1 egg	
	parsley, thyme and chives	
	salt, freshly ground pepper	
	SAUCE	
50g/2 oz	butter	¼ cup
	1 large onion, chopped	
	1 large carrot, chopped	
225g/8 oz	prepared mixed vegetables	½ lb
450ml/¾ pint	beef stock	2 cups
150ml/¼ pint	red wine	⅔ cup
1 × 15ml spoon/ 1 tablespoon	butter	1 tablespoon
1 × 15ml spoon/ 1 tablespoon	flour	1 tablespoon

Make the stuffing first. Melt the butter in a pan, and cook the shallot and garlic until soft. Mix together all the stuffing ingredients.

Lay the slices of beef flat, and spread them with mustard and seasoning. Spread with the stuffing, roll up, turning the sides over so that the stuffing is enclosed. Tie securely.

To prepare the sauce, melt the butter in a pan, and brown the onion slightly. Add the other vegetables, and stir together. Put into a large ovenproof dish and lay the meat on top. Pour in the stock and wine, then cover and cook in a moderate oven, 180°C/350°F/Gas 4, for 1½ hours. Remove the lid after 30 minutes, and turn the meat parcels over after 1 hour.

Transfer the beef olives to a warmed serving dish, and cut off the thread. Arrange the vegetables around the meat. Strain the cooking liquor into a pan, then boil until it is reduced.

Knead together the butter and flour to a smooth paste, and add this, off heat, to the sauce in small pieces, stirring until dissolved. Heat until the sauce thickens, then pour some of it over the meat, and serve the rest in a sauce-boat.

Fondue Bourguignonne

Metric/imperial		American
175g/6 oz	good quality fillet (filet mignon) or rump steak per person, cut into 2.5cm/1 inch cubes	⅓ lb
	garlic, grated	
	salt, freshly ground pepper	
	oil for deep frying	
	SAUCES	
	Sauce Béarnaise (page 76)	
	Sauce Hollandaise (page 77)	
	Sauce Tartare (page 78)	

Season the meat with the garlic, and with salt and pepper. Fill the fondue pot one-third full of oil, and heat it to 190°C/375°F. If possible, have a second pot of oil heating so that the first pot, in use on the dining-table, can be replaced when it cools. Carry the first pot carefully to the table.

At the table, light the spirit lamp or burner, and put the pot on the trivet. If using an electric table cooker, fill it one-third full of oil, set the thermostat, and heat it up at the table itself. Bring the meat and the sauces to the table, arrange the sauces round the fondue pot in the centre, and place a dish of meat and two long-handled forks in front of each diner. The diner spears a piece of meat on a fork, dips it into the hot oil and holds it there until cooked. After cooking, he transfers the meat to the second, cold fork and dips it into one or other of the sauces before eating.

This dish is given much of its character by the side dishes served with it. Choose accompaniments from among the following: beetroot (beet) sliced in vinegar, chopped celery, chopped nuts, cocktail onions, cucumber in soured cream or thick yoghurt sprinkled with dill, green salad with vinaigrette, sliced gherkins, sliced potato in vinaigrette, sliced tomato with chives and vinaigrette. French bread and butter should also be served.

Fondue Bourguignonne

Blanquette de Veau à L'Ancienne

(Veal Stew with Mushrooms and Onions)

SERVES 6

Metric/imperial		American
900g/2 lb	stewing (boneless) veal, cut into 5cm/2 inch pieces	2 lb
	2 cloves	
	1 large onion	
	1 large carrot, cut into quarters lengthways	
	1 clove of garlic, crushed	
	salt, freshly ground pepper	
	bouquet garni	
25g/1 oz	butter	2 tablespoons
25g/1 oz	flour	$\frac{1}{4}$ cup
10 × 5ml spoons/ 10 teaspoons	double (heavy) cream	10 teaspoons
	8–12 button (pickling) onions	
	8–12 button mushrooms	
	lemon juice	
	ground nutmeg	
	GARNISH chopped parsley	
	fleurons (page 79)	

Soak the veal in cold water for 30 minutes. Press the cloves into the onion. Put the meat into fresh cold water, heat to boiling point, then simmer for 10 minutes. Skim well and drain. Transfer to a clean pan with 1.2litres/2 pints/5 US cups water, the onion, carrot, garlic, seasoning and bouquet garni. Heat gently to boiling point, then skim, half cover and simmer very slowly for $1\frac{1}{4}$–$1\frac{1}{2}$ hours or until the veal is just tender (not soft). Remove the onion, carrot and bouquet garni. Strain the stock for making the sauce. Cover the pan and keep the meat hot.

Melt the butter in a pan, stir in the flour, and cook together for 3 minutes without colouring the flour. Gradually add the reserved stock from the veal, stirring all the time, and cook gently until the sauce thickens. Add the cream and seasoning if required, and pour the sauce over the meat in the pan.

Cook the button (pickling) onions in lightly salted water for 6 minutes. Drain, then add them to the stew. Simmer the mushrooms separately in water with a little lemon juice for 3 minutes, then add them with their cooking liquid to the stew, and stir in gently.

Re-heat the stew gently almost to boiling point. Add the nutmeg, and season to taste. Serve very hot, sprinkled with chopped parsley and garnished with *fleurons*.

Agneau Reine Claude

(Grilled Lamb with Greengage Sauce)

Metric/imperial		American
	8 trimmed lamb cutlets (rib chops)	
	salt, freshly ground pepper	
1 × 15ml spoon/ 1 tablespoon	fresh rosemary, chopped	1 tablespoon
	2 shallots, thinly sliced	
	1 clove of garlic, crushed	
200ml/$\frac{1}{3}$ pint	red wine	$\frac{7}{8}$ cup
225g/8 oz	greengages, halved and stoned (pitted)	$\frac{1}{2}$ lb
2 × 15ml spoons/ 2 tablespoons	brandy	3 tablespoons
	GARNISH $\frac{1}{2}$ lemon, flesh scooped out	
	redcurrant jelly	
	strips of lemon rind	
	sprigs fresh rosemary	

Put the lamb cutlets into a shallow dish. Add salt and pepper to taste, the rosemary, shallots, garlic and the wine. Cover and marinate in a refrigerator for 6 hours.

Remove the cutlets from their marinade. Strain the marinade into a saucepan and add the greengages. Simmer gently until the greengages are quite tender, then sieve the sauce, and add the brandy.

Grill (broil) the lamb cutlets until sealed on the outside but still pink in the centre. Heat the sauce gently, and fill the lemon with redcurrant jelly. Top with the strips of lemon rind.

Spoon the sauce over or around the cutlets, and garnish with the lemon and with sprigs of rosemary.

Agneau Reine Claude

Navarin D'Agneau Printanier

(Lamb Stew with Vegetables)

SERVES 8–9

Metric/imperial		American
50g/2 oz	flour	½ cup
	salt, freshly ground pepper	
1.15kg/2½ lb	shoulder of lamb, boned and cut into 2.5cm/1 inch cubes	2½ lb
10 × 5ml spoons/ 10 teaspoons	cooking oil	10 teaspoons
	1 small onion, chopped	
	4 tomatoes, skinned and chopped	
50g/2 oz	concentrated tomato purée (paste)	¼ cup
	bouquet garni	
1 × 5ml spoon/ 1 teaspoon	dried herbs (basil, mint, oregano)	1 teaspoon
900ml/1½ pints (approx)	beef stock	3¾ cups (approx)
	1 clove of garlic, crushed	
225g/8 oz	new potatoes, cut into oval shapes	½ lb
225g/8 oz	small young (early) carrots, cut into oval shapes	½ lb
225g/8 oz	small young turnips, cut into oval shapes	½ lb
	8 button (pickling) onions	
	butter and oil	
100g/4 oz	French (green) beans, cut into diamond shapes	¼ lb
100g/4 oz	fresh peas	¾ cup

GARNISH
chopped parsley

Season the flour with salt and pepper, and use some of it to dust the meat cubes. Heat the oil in a frying pan (skillet), and brown the meat on all sides. Add the onion, and fry gently for 1 minute. Sprinkle in the remaining flour, and cook until it is nut-brown.

Transfer the mixture to a large flameproof casserole. Add the chopped tomatoes, the purée (paste), bouquet garni, herbs and stock, and season well. Add the garlic with any juices in the frying pan (skillet), heat gently to boiling point, then cover closely and simmer for 1½ hours. Skim off any excess fat from time to time during cooking.

Meanwhile, put the potatoes, carrots and turnips into boiling salted water, and cook gently for 10 minutes. Add them to the stew 10–20 minutes before the end of the cooking time, so that they will be tender when the meat is ready. Sauté the onions in butter and oil until lightly browned on all sides, and add them to the stew about 15 minutes before the end of the cooking time. Blanch the beans and peas in a little boiling salted water until tender. Drain, then add them to the stew 3–4 minutes before the end of the cooking time, reserved a few peas for garnishing.

When the lamb is ready, skim off any excess fat. Remove any loose bones and the bouquet garni. Transfer the stew to a warmed serving dish, and sprinkle with the chopped parsley and reserved peas just before serving.

Gigot Boulangère

(Roast Leg of Lamb with Baked Potatoes)

SERVES 12

Metric/imperial		American
1.15kg/2½ lb	leg of lamb	2½ lb
	2 cloves garlic	
50g/2 oz	butter	¼ cup
25g/1 oz	lard (shortening)	2 tablespoons
	salt, freshly ground pepper	
150ml/¼ pint	stock	⅔ cup
225g/8 oz	onions, thinly sliced	½ lb
450g/1 lb	potatoes, peeled and sliced	1 lb
	bouquet garni	

Ask the butcher to cut the knuckle off the leg of lamb. Make six small slits in the flesh. Skin the garlic cloves and cut each into three slivers. Insert one sliver in each slit. Blend together the butter and lard (shortening), and spread half over the joint. Season well. Place the meat in a roasting tin (pan), and roast in a fairly hot oven, 200°C/400°F/Gas 6, for 45 minutes, basting the meat from time to time with some of the stock.

Heat the remaining butter and lard (shortening) in a second roasting tin (pan), and sauté the onions until soft and lightly coloured. Add the potatoes and bouquet garni. Spread the onions and potatoes in the tin, and place the half-roasted meat on top. reduce the heat to 190°C/375°F /Gas 5, and roast for a further 45 minutes, basting from time to time, with the juices form the first roasting tin (pan). Remove the joint when fully cooked, carve into thick slices and keep hot. Increase the heat to fairly hot, 200°C/400°F/ Gas 6, and continue cooking the potatoes and onions for about 15 minutes until lightly browned.

Arrange the meat, potatoes and onions in a serving dish. Scrape and pour any juices from both tins into a saucepan. Add any remaining stock, and boil gently for 5 minutes to reduce the sauce. Skim, then pour into a warmed sauce-boat. Serve with the meat and vegetables.

Cassoulet de Toulouse

(Haricot Bean Stew with Pork and Lamb)

SERVES 10–12

Metric/imperial		American
900g/2 lb	haricot (navy) beans	2 lb
900g/2 lb	goose or duck (½ or ¼ bird)	2 lb
450g/1 lb	boned pork	1 lb
225g/8 oz	pork rind	½ lb
225–450g/½–1 lb	boiling bacon (smoked shoulder roll)	½–1 lb
350g/12 oz	onions	¾ lb
	1 bouquet garni, including ½ head unpeeled garlic, 2 cloves and 2 bay leaves	
	salt, freshly ground pepper	
4 × 15ml spoons/ 4 tablespoons	pork, goose or duck fat (from roasting bird)	5 tablespoons
900g/2 lb	boned well-aged lamb, cut into 5cm/2 inch cubes	2 lb
450g/1 lb	lamb and/or pork bones	1 lb
	4–5 cloves garlic	
6 × 15ml spoons/ 6 tablespoons	concentrated tomato purée (paste)	7 tablespoons
600ml/1 pint	dry white wine	2½ cups
1.2 litres/2 pints	stock	5 cups
675g/1½ lb	coarse-cut garlic sausage, cut into 5cm/2 inch lengths	1½ lb
225g/8 oz	dry white bread-crumbs or as required	2 cups
	extra pork, goose or duck fat	

Soak the haricot (navy) beans overnight in cold water. Roast the goose or duck and the boned pork until just cooked. Cool, reserving the cooking juices and fat, then cut the goose or duck into serving portions and the pork into 5cm/2 inch cubes. Meanwhile, blanch the pork rind in boiling water for 2 minutes, then cut it into 6mm/¼ inch dice, and simmer in fresh water for 15 minutes.

Put the drained beans and the pork rind into a large stewpan with enough water to cover them. Add the boiling bacon. Skin and slice 100g/4 oz/¼ US lb onions and add them with the bouquet garni. Season with salt. Boil briskly for at least 10 minutes, then skim well, reduce the heat and simmer for 2–2½ hours or until the beans are tender. Add extra boiling water during cooking, if required. Do not cover the pan. Remove and slice the bacon; discard the bouquet garni.

Put just enough of the pork, goose or duck fat into a flameproof casserole to cover the bottom to a depth of 6mm/¼ inch. Heat well, and brown the cubes of lamb on all sides. Remove, then put to one side. Brown the bones in a little more of the fat, then remove and put to one side. Skin and chop all the remaining onions, and fry them in the same fat for 5 minutes until lightly browned. Return the meat and bones to the casserole. Add the garlic, with the tomato purée (paste), wine and stock, and season to taste. Bring to simmering point, cover and simmer for 1½ hours. Remove the meat and discard the bones. Strain the cooking liquid into a bowl and add any pan juices kept from roasting the goose, duck and boneless pork. Skim off any excess fat, and put to one side.

Drain the beans and rind, and add their cooking liquid to the liquid and pan juices in the bowl. Put a layer of beans and rind in the bottom of a very large flameproof casserole or pot. Cover with layers of goose or duck, lamb, bacon and sausage. Repeat the layers until the ingredients are used, ending with beans. Pour in enough of the cooking liquid from the bowl to cover all but the top layer of beans, then cover thickly with breadcrumbs, and dot with extra fat.

Bring the casserole or pot to simmering point, then cook, uncovered, in a moderate oven, 180°C/350°F/Gas 4, for 30 minutes. Break up the breadcrumb crust, and baste it with the liquid which wells up. Continue cooking, basting several times, for another 40 minutes. Serve from the casserole.

Cassoulet de Toulouse

Tripes à la Mode de Caen

(Tripe with Pork in Cider)

Metric/imperial		American
	1 calf's foot	
	1 pig's trotter (foot)	
75g/3 oz	pickled (salt) pork	3 oz
	4 whole cloves	
	2 large onions, halved	
	3 carrots, thinly sliced	
	2 cloves garlic	
	salt, freshly ground pepper	
	Cayenne pepper	
450–675g/1–1½ lb	dressed calf's (ready-to-cook honeycomb) tripe, cut into 7.5cm/3 inch pieces	1–1½ lb
	bouquet garni	
	6 peppercorns	
200ml/⅓ pint	dry (hard) still cider	⅞ cup
5 × 15ml spoons/5 tablespoons	Calvados (applejack)	6 tablespoons
	cornflour (cornstarch)	

Ask the butcher to clean the calf's foot and pig's trotter (foot) and to chop them into two or three pieces each. Remove the rind from the pork. Put to one side and dice the meat. Press one clove into each half onion.

Use a deep pot or casserole, preferably earthenware, with a tight-fitting lid. In the bottom, put the pork rind, then a layer of carrots, two half onions, one clove of garlic, the calf's foot, the trotter (pig's foot), and half the pork meat. Season well with salt, pepper and Cayenne pepper, and cover with half the tripe. Put in the rest of the carrots and onions, the second garlic clove, the rest of the pork meat and the tripe. Add the bouquet garni and peppercorns, and season to taste. Pour in the cider and Calvados (applejack), then cover the pot very tightly, and cook in a warm oven, 160°C/325°F/Gas 3, for 6–7 hours.

Transfer the tripe, pork meat and carrots to a warmed serving dish, and keep hot. Strain the stock, discarding the calf's foot and trotter (pig's foot), the bouquet garni, peppercorns, onions and garlic. Measure the liquid. For each 300ml/½ pint/1¼ US cups liquid, blend 1 × 2.5ml spoon/½ teaspoon cornflour (cornstarch) with 1 × 15ml spoon/1 tablespoon water. Add a little of the hot liquid, and stir gently over low heat until the sauce thickens slightly and is very hot. Season to taste, and pour the sauce over the tripe. Serve at once.

Poulet Chasseur

(Chicken Chasseur)

SERVES 4–6

Metric/imperial		American
25g/1 oz	flour	¼ cup
	salt, freshly ground pepper	
	1 roasting (roaster) chicken, divided into 8 serving portions	
1 × 15ml spoon/1 tablespoon	cooking oil	1 tablespoon
50g/2 oz	butter	¼ cup
25g/1 oz	onion or shallot, chopped	¼ cup
175g/6 oz	button mushrooms, sliced	1½ cups
150ml/¼ pint	dry white wine	⅔ cup
	3 tomatoes, chopped	
300ml/½ pint	chicken stock	1¼ cups
	1 sprig each of fresh tarragon, chervil and parsley, chopped	

Season the flour with salt and pepper, and use to dust the chicken portions. Heat the oil and butter in a frying pan (skillet), and fry the chicken pieces until tender and browned all over, allowing 15–20 minutes for dark meat (drumsticks and thighs), 10–12 minutes for light meat (breast and wings). When tender, remove from the pan, drain on soft kitchen paper, and transfer to a warmed serving dish. Cover loosely with buttered paper and keep hot.

Put the onion or shallot into the pan, in the fat in which the chicken was cooked, and fry gently without colouring. Add the mushrooms to the pan, and continue frying until tender. Pour in the wine, and add the chopped tomatoes and the stock. Stir until well blended, then simmer gently for 10 minutes. Add most of the herbs to the sauce, and season to taste.

Pour the sauce over the chicken, sprinkle with the remaining herbs, and serve very hot.

Poulet à la King

(Chicken à la King)

Metric/imperial		American
50g/2 oz	butter	¼ cup
	1 red pepper, de-seeded and thinly sliced	
175g/6 oz	button mushrooms, sliced	1½ cups
350–450g/¾–1 lb	cooked chicken, diced	¾–1 lb
4 × 15ml spoons/ 4 tablespoons	whisky	5 tablespoons
	salt, freshly ground pepper	
	a pinch of garlic powder	
200ml/⅓ pint	double (heavy) cream	⅞ cup
	1 egg yolk	

Melt 25g/1 oz/2 US tablespoons of the butter in a frying pan (skillet), and, when foaming, add the pepper, and fry quickly for 2–3 minutes. Stir in the mushrooms, and cook gently for another 2 minutes. Put to one side.

In a second pan, melt the remaining butter, add the diced chicken, and fry gently, turning as required, until well heated through. Pour on the whisky, ignite, and shake the pan to distribute the flames. When they die down, season the chicken well with salt, pepper and garlic powder, and simmer until nearly all the juices have evaporated. Stir in most of the cream, then bring gently to boiling point, stirring all the time. Blend the egg yolk into the remaining cream, and add a little of the cooking liquid from the pepper and mushrooms. Add the pepper and mushrooms to the chicken, then stir in the blended yolk and cream. Re-heat gently without boiling until the sauce thickens a little. Pile on to a warmed serving dish, and serve surrounded by a ring of cooked rice.

Coq au Vin

SERVES 4–6

Metric/imperial		American
	1 chicken, jointed (cut up) with giblets	
	bouquet garni	
	salt, freshly ground pepper	
50g/2 oz	unsalted butter	¼ cup
1 × 15ml spoon/ 1 tablespoon	oil	1 tablespoon
125g/5 oz	green (Canadian) bacon rashers (slices), without rinds and chopped	generous ½ cup
125g/5 oz	button (pickling) onions	generous ¼ lb
2 × 15ml spoons/ 2 tablespoons	brandy	3 tablespoons
600ml/1 pint	Burgundy wine	2½ cups
175g/6 oz	button mushrooms	1½ cups
	1 clove of garlic, crushed	
2 × 5ml spoons/ 2 teaspoons	concentrated tomato purée (paste)	2 teaspoons
25g/1 oz	butter	2 tablespoons
25g/1 oz	flour	¼ cup
GARNISH		
	croûtes of fried bread	
	chopped parsley	

Place the giblets in a saucepan, cover with water, and add the bouquet garni, salt and pepper. Cook gently for 1 hour to make stock.

Heat the unsalted butter and the oil in a flameproof casserole, add the bacon and the onions, and cook slowly until the fat runs and the onions are lightly coloured. Remove them to a plate.

Brown the chicken lightly all over in the same fat, then pour off any surplus fat. Warm the brandy, set alight, and pour it over the chicken. When the flame dies down, add the wine, stock, bacon, onions, mushrooms, garlic and tomato purée (paste). Cover and cook in a cool oven, 150°C/300°F/Gas 2, for 1 hour or until the chicken is tender. Transfer the chicken to a serving dish and keep hot. Using a perforated spoon, remove the onions, bacon and mushrooms, and arrange over the chicken.

Simmer the liquid in the casserole until reduced by about one third. Knead together the 25g/1 oz/2 US tablespoons butter and the flour to form a paste, and add this, off heat, to the sauce in small pieces, stirring until dissolved. Heat until the sauce thickens, stirring frequently.

Pour the sauce over the chicken, arrange croûtes of fried bread round the dish, and sprinkle with chopped parsley.

Coq au Vin

Poulet Vallée D'Auge

(Chicken in Cider and Cream Sauce)

Metric/imperial		American
	1 roasting (roaster) chicken, trussed	
	salt, freshly ground pepper	
	ground nutmeg	
8 × 5ml spoons/ 8 teaspoons	butter	8 teaspoons
4 × 5ml spoons/ 4 teaspoons	cooking oil	4 teaspoons
	1 leek, white part only, thickly sliced	
	1 carrot, thickly sliced	
	2 small onions, chopped	
	2 sticks celery, sliced	
4 × 5ml spoons/ 4 teaspoons	Calvados (applejack)	4 teaspoons
150ml/¼ pint	dry (hard) still cider	⅔ cup
150ml/¼ pint	chicken stock	⅔ cup
	bouquet garni	
	2 egg yolks	
1 × 5ml spoon/ 1 teaspoon	cornflour (cornstarch)	1 teaspoon
150ml/¼ pint	single (light) cream	⅔ cup
	GARNISH sautéed button mushrooms	
	lemon juice	

Season the chicken inside with salt, pepper and nutmeg. Heat 4 × 5ml spoons/4 teaspoons butter and all the oil in a frying pan (skillet), add the leek, carrot and onions, cover and cook over very gentle heat until lightly browned, stirring all the time. Put the vegetables into a large casserole which will hold the chicken. Spread the remaining butter on the breast of the chicken, and place it in the casserole. Cover and cook in a fairly hot oven, 190°C/375°F/Gas 5, for 20 minutes, then add the celery, Calvados (applejack), cider, stock and bouquet garni, and season to taste. Cover and cook in the oven for a further 30 minutes. Remove the chicken and cut into quarters or serving portions. Place in an ovenproof baking dish, cover loosely with buttered greaseproof (waxed) paper or foil and keep hot. Strain the liquid into a saucepan, heat slowly to boiling point, then boil for 10 minutes or until well reduced.

Beat the yolks with the cornflour (cornstarch) until blended, then stir in the cream. Remove the sauce from the heat, and stir a little into the egg yolk mixture. Add the egg yolk mixture slowly to the rest of the sauce, beating vigorously. Season to taste, and pour the sauce over the chicken. Garnish with the mushrooms sprinkled with lemon juice.

Canard à L'Orange

(Duck with Orange)

SERVES 4–5

Metric/imperial		American
	1 duck, trussed	
	fat for basting	
2 × 15ml spoons/ 2 tablespoons	flour	3 tablespoons
300ml/½ pint	stock	1¼ cups
	salt, freshly ground pepper	
	STUFFING	
50g/2 oz	butter	¼ cup
100g/4 oz	fresh breadcrumbs	2 cups
	a pinch of ground nutmeg	
1 × 5ml spoon/ 1 tablespoon	fresh parsley, chopped	1 tablespoon
1 × 5ml spoon/ 1 teaspoon	fresh mixed herbs, chopped	1 teaspoon
	grated rind of ½ lemon	
	salt, freshly ground pepper	
	1 egg, beaten	
	GARNISH slices and pared rind of 1 large orange	
1 × 15ml spoon/ 1 tablespoon	brandy	1 tablespoon

Prepare the stuffing first. Melt the butter in a pan, and mix with the breadcrumbs. Add the nutmeg, herbs and lemon rind. Season to taste, then stir in the egg to bind the stuffing.

Fill the duck with the stuffing, then heat the fat, and baste the duck well. Roast in a fairly hot oven, 200°C/400°F/Gas 6, covered with buttered paper, for 1–1½ hours or until tender, basting frequently. Uncover for the last 30 minutes. Keep hot.

Pour off the fat from the roasting tin (pan), sprinkle in the flour, and brown it. Stir in the stock, simmer for 3–4 minutes, then season to taste, and strain. Remove the trussing string from the duck.

Meanwhile, soak the orange slices in the brandy. Cut the rind into thin strips, boil in a little water for 5 minutes, then drain. Heat the orange slices gently in the brandy.

Garnish the cooked duck with the strips of rind and hot orange slices, and serve with the sauce.

Canard à L'Orange

42

EGGS AND CHEESE

Pipérade Basque

(Scrambled Eggs with Vegetables)

Metric/imperial		American
50g/2 oz	butter	¼ cup
	2 red or green peppers, de-seeded and thinly sliced	
	2 onions, thinly sliced	
	1 clove of garlic, crushed	
450g/1 lb	tomatoes, skinned and roughly chopped	1 lb
	salt, freshly ground pepper	
	6 eggs	
3 × 15ml spoons/ 3 tablespoons	milk	4 tablespoons

Melt the butter in a pan and fry the peppers for about 5 minutes, then add the onions and garlic, and continue cooking gently for 5 minutes until softened. Add the tomatoes, and cook for a further 2–3 minutes. Season generously. Beat the eggs lightly together with the milk, and when the vegetables are mushy, pour in the eggs. Reduce the heat and cook gently, stirring all the time, until just set and creamy. Serve at once with chunks of bread.

Omelette Fines Herbes

(Herb Omelet)

SERVES 1

Metric/imperial		American
	2 eggs	
	salt, freshly ground pepper	
1 × 2.5ml spoon/ ½ teaspoon	fresh tarragon, chopped	½ teaspoon
1 × 2.5ml spoon/ ½ teaspoon	fresh chervil, chopped	½ teaspoon
1 × 5ml spoon/ 1 teaspoon	fresh parsley, chopped	1 teaspoon
	chopped chives	
1 × 15ml spoon/ 1 tablespoon	water	1 tablespoon
1 × 15ml spoon/ 1 tablespoon	unsalted butter	1 tablespoon

Break the eggs into a basin, season with salt and pepper, add the herbs and water, and beat lightly with a fork.

Place the pan over gentle heat and, when it is hot, add the butter. Tilt the pan so that the whole surface is greased lightly. Pour in the beaten eggs, then leave for 10 seconds. With the back of the prongs of a fork, or with a spatula, draw the mixture gently from the sides to the centre as it sets, and let the liquid egg from the centre run to the sides. Repeat as necessary, without stirring. Leave to cook for a further 4–5 seconds until the omelet is golden underneath. Remove the pan from the heat, and loosen the edges of the omelet with a round-bladed knife. Fold the omelet over so that both edges fold into the centre, then tip on to a plate with the folded sides underneath.

Pipérade Basque

Oeufs en Cocottes

(Eggs in Cocottes)

Metric/imperial		American
25g/1 oz	butter	2 tablespoons
	4 eggs	
	salt, freshly ground pepper	
4 × 15ml spoons/ 4 tablespoons	single (light) cream	5 tablespoons
	ground nutmeg	

Butter four ramekins or cocottes at least 2.5cm/1 inch deep, and stand them in a baking tin (pan) containing enough warm water to come half-way up their sides. Break an egg into each warm dish, and season with salt and pepper. Top with any remaining butter cut into flakes and with the cream. Sprinkle with the nutmeg. Bake in a moderate oven, 180°C/350°F/Gas 4, for 6–10 minutes, depending on the thickness of the dishes. The whites of the eggs should be just set. Serve at once.

Oeufs Parmentier

(Parmentier Eggs)

Metric/imperial		American
675g/1½ lb	potatoes, peeled and cut into small pieces	1½ lb
100g/4 oz	blue Brie, finely chopped	1 cup
	salt, freshly ground pepper	
2 × 15ml spoons/ 2 tablespoons	milk	3 tablespoons
	4 eggs	

Cook the potatoes in boiling salted water for 10–15 minutes until tender, then drain and mash. Add most of the cheese, the salt, pepper and the milk, then beat with a wooden spoon until creamy.

Using a forcing (pastry) bag with a large star nozzle (tube), pipe four nests of potato on to a greased baking sheet. Break an egg into each nest, then sprinkle the remaining cheese over the eggs. Bake in a fairly hot oven, 190°C/375°F/Gas 5, for 12–15 minutes until the egg whites are lightly set and the potato is browned.

Oeufs Belle Hélène

(Poached Eggs with Asparagus Sauce)

SERVES 6–8

Metric/imperial		American
	50 heads asparagus	
600ml/1 pint	milk	2½ cups
	1 large lettuce, finely shredded	
	1 medium onion, chopped	
	1 bay leaf	
	3 sprigs thyme	
	salt, freshly ground pepper	
50g/2 oz	butter	¼ cup
50g/2 oz	flour	½ cup
	7–9 eggs	
1 × 5ml spoon/ 1 teaspoon	lemon juice	1 teaspoon

Scrape the white stalks of the asparagus and cut off and reserve the points. Put the milk into a saucepan and bring to the boil. Add the lettuce and onion together with the bay leaf, thyme and a little salt, then put in the asparagus stalks. Simmer gently for about 15 minutes or until the stalks are tender.

Drain the asparagus, and rub through a sieve. Melt the butter in a second pan, add the flour and cook for 1 minute. Remove from the heat and stir in the asparagus purée. Return to the heat and bring to the boil, stirring all the time until the sauce thickens. Beat one of the eggs lightly, stir it into the sauce and continue stirring over very gentle heat, without boiling, until the sauce is very thick. Season the sauce well and add the lemon juice.

Cook the reserved asparagus points in boiling salted water for 5 minutes or until tender, then drain well.

Poach the remaining eggs, and trim neatly to a round shape. Chop the trimmings finely and add them to the sauce. Spoon it in a line down the centre of a heated serving dish. Arrange an equal number of eggs on each side, and garnish the top of the sauce, between the eggs, with the asparagus points.

Oeufs Courtet

Oeufs Courtet

(Eggs Courtet)

Metric/imperial		American
	4 tomatoes	
	4 eggs	
4 × 15ml spoons/ 4 tablespoons	milk	5 tablespoons
	salt, freshly ground pepper	
25g/1 oz	butter	2 tablespoons
150ml/¼ pint	aspic jelly	⅔ cup
	GARNISH	
	lettuce leaves	
	chopped parsley	

Cut the tomatoes in half and scoop out the centres. Leave upside-down to drain. Beat together lightly the eggs, milk, salt and pepper. Melt the butter in a small pan, add the beaten egg, reduce the heat and cook gently, stirring all the time, until the eggs are just set and creamy. Fill the tomato cups with the eggs, and leave until cold.

Melt the aspic jelly, then chill it until at setting point but still liquid. Coat each filled tomato half with the jelly. Chill the remaining jelly until set, then chop it roughly.

Serve the tomato cups surrounded by the chopped jelly on a bed of lettuce, and garnish with chopped parsley.

Soufflé au Camembert

Metric/imperial		American
100g/4 oz	ripe Camembert, crusts removed	¼ lb
100g/4 oz	curd cheese	½ cup
2 × 5ml spoons/ 2 teaspoons	gelatine (unflavored gelatin)	2 teaspoons
150ml/¼ pint	skimmed milk	⅔ cup
	salt	
	2 egg whites	

Sieve or mash the cheeses until both are smooth and well blended. Soften the gelatine in the milk in a small heatproof container, then stand the container in a pan of hot water, and stir until the gelatine has dissolved. Leave to cool, then mix with the cheeses and seasoning. Chill.

Whisk the egg whites until stiff but not dry. When the cheese mixture is beginning to set at the edges, fold in the egg whites lightly but thoroughly. Turn into a wetted 600ml/1 pint/2½ US cup souffle dish, and chill until set.

Croque Monsieur

(Ham and Cheese Sandwich)

butter	
8 slices white bread, crusts removed	
4 thin slices cooked ham	
4 slices Gruyère cheese	

Butter one side of each slice of bread. Trim the ham and the cheese to fit the bread, and make four sandwiches with a filling of one thin layer of ham and one of cheese. Spread one side of each sandwich with butter. Grease a shallow baking dish or tin (pan), large enough to hold the sandwiches in one layer, and place the tin in the oven. Heat to moderate, 180°C/350°F/Gas 4. Place the sandwiches in the hot tin, buttered side up, and return to the oven. Bake for 10 minutes until golden and crisp on top.

Croque Monsieur

Pâté de Fromage

(Cheese Pâté)

SERVES 6–8

Metric/imperial		American
100g/4 oz	Roquefort cheese, crumbled	1 cup
100g/4 oz	cream cheese	½ cup
1 × 15ml spoon/ 1 tablespoon	softened butter	1 tablespoon
100g/4 oz	Comté cheese, finely grated	1 cup
75g/3 oz	walnuts, finely chopped	¾ cup
1 × 2.5ml spoon/ ½ teaspoon	Worcestershire sauce	½ teaspoon
1 × 2.5ml spoon/ ½ teaspoon	paprika	½ teaspoon
	a pinch of Cayenne pepper	
	chopped parsley	
	lettuce leaves	

Blend together the Roquefort, cream cheese and butter with the back of a spoon, then work in the Comté cheese. Add the walnuts with the Worcestershire sauce, paprika and Cayenne pepper, and mix well. Shape the cheese mixture into a ball, and roll in enough parsley to cover completely. Cover with clingfilm (plastic wrap), and chill.

Serve in small wedges on lettuce leaves, with slices of Melba toast.

Ramekins de Fromage

(Cheese Ramekins)

Metric/imperial		American
10 × 5ml spoons/10 teaspoons (approx)	milk	10 teaspoons (approx)
25g/1 oz (approx)	fresh white breadcrumbs	½ cup (approx)
25g/1 oz	Emmental cheese, finely grated	¼ cup
25g/1 oz	Parmesan cheese, grated	¼ cup
25g/1 oz	softened unsalted butter	2 tablespoons
	1 egg, separated	
	salt, freshly ground pepper	
	a pinch of ground mace (optional)	

Heat the milk, and pour just enough over the breadcrumbs to cover them. Leave to stand for 5–10 minutes. Stir in both cheeses and the butter, then mix with the egg yolk. Season well with salt, pepper and mace, if used. Whisk the egg white until very stiff. Stir one spoonful into the cheese mixture, then fold in the rest. Turn the mixture into four small greased ramekins, and bake in a fairly hot oven, 200°C/400°F/Gas 6, for 15–20 minutes until risen and slightly browned. Serve at once.

Gougère

(Choux Pastry with Cheese)

SERVES 6

Metric/imperial		American
450ml/¾ pint	water	2 cups
75g/3 oz	butter	6 tablespoons
	salt, freshly ground pepper	
175g/6 oz	flour, sifted	1½ cups
	2½ egg yolks	
	3 eggs	
175g/6 oz	Gruyère cheese	scant ⅓ lb

Put the water, butter, salt and pepper in a pan, and bring to
the boil. Remove from the heat and add the flour all at
once. Return to the heat and beat well with a wooden
spoon until the mixture forms a smooth paste which leaves
the sides of the pan clean. Remove from the heat, cool
slightly, add 1½ egg yolks, and beat well. Add the whole
eggs, one at a time, beating thoroughly between each
addition.

Dice half the cheese and grate the rest. Reserve about
25g/1 oz/¼ US cup of each and put to one side. Mix the rest
lightly into the pastry. Using a small round or oval spoon,
place large spoonfuls of the mixture side by side in a circle
all round a shallow greased 17.5cm/7 inch sandwich tin
(layer cake pan). Make a second circle just inside the first,
and repeat until the dish is full. Make the last central choux
rather bigger than the rest. Beat the remaining yolk with a
little water, and brush the tops of the choux with it.
Sprinkle with the reserved cheese. Bake in a fairly hot oven,
190°C/375°F/Gas 5, for 30–35 minutes, until risen and
golden-brown. Serve hot or cold.

Gougère

VEGETABLES AND SALADS

Pommes Lyonnaise

Pommes Lyonnaise

(Lyonnaise Potatoes)

SERVES 6

Metric/imperial		American
900g/2 lb	potatoes	2 lb
75g/3 oz	butter	6 tablespoons
225g/8 oz	onions, thinly sliced	½ lb
	salt, freshly ground pepper	
	chopped parsley	

Boil or steam the potatoes in their skins until tender, then drain, peel and cut into slices 6mm/¼ inch thick.

Melt the butter in a frying pan (skillet), and fry the onions gently until just golden. Remove from the pan, put to one side, and keep warm. Add the potatoes to the pan, and fry on both sides until crisp and golden. Replace the onions in the pan, and mix with the potatoes. Season to taste with salt and pepper, then turn into a serving dish, and sprinkle with the parsley.

Pommes Parisienne

(Parisienne Potatoes)

SERVES 4–6

Metric/imperial		American
25g/1 oz	butter	2 tablespoons
1 × 15ml spoon/ 1 tablespoon	oil	1 tablespoon
900g/2 lb	potatoes, peeled, cut into small rounds and dried (see Note)	2 lb
	salt, freshly ground pepper	
3 × 15ml spoons/ 3 tablespoons	softened butter	4 tablespoons
3 × 15ml spoons/ 3 tablespoons	fresh mixed herbs, finely chopped	4 tablespoons

Heat the 25g/1 oz/2 US tablespoons butter and the oil in a frying pan (skillet) large enough to hold all the potatoes in one layer. Put in the potatoes, coat evenly in the fat, then fry gently until a light golden colour. Reduce the heat, sprinkle with the salt, and cover the pan. Continue frying very gently for 12–15 minutes, shaking the pan frequently, until the potatoes are tender. Drain off the fat. Raise the heat, and shake the potatoes in the pan until sizzling. Remove from the heat, add the softened butter and the herbs, season well with pepper, and roll the potatoes round the pan until coated with herbs. Arrange round a meat dish or serve separately in a warmed dish.

Note Cut the potatoes into rounds with a potato ball scoop.

Pommes Parisienne

Pommes Dauphine

(Dauphine Potatoes)

SERVES 4–6

Metric/imperial		American
450g/1 lb	potatoes	1 lb
	salt, freshly ground pepper	
	oil for deep frying	
	CHOUX PASTRY	
200ml/⅓ pint	water	⅞ cup
40g/1½ oz	butter	3 tablespoons
	a pinch of salt	
75g/3 oz	flour, sifted	¾ cup
	¾ egg yolk	
	1½ eggs	

Prepare the choux pastry first. Put the water, butter and salt in a pan, and bring to the boil. Remove from the heat and add the flour all at once. Return to the heat and beat well with a wooden spoon until the mixture forms a smooth paste which leaves the sides of the pan clean. Remove from the heat, cool slightly, add the egg yolk, and beat well. Add the 1½ eggs, separately, and beat thoroughly between each addition.

Meanwhile, boil or steam the potatoes until tender, then drain thoroughly, peel and sieve. Season well with salt and pepper.

Beat the potato purée into the choux pastry, then mould the mixture into quenelle shapes with two dessertspoons. Drop spoonfuls into deep fat, a few at a time, and cook until they are golden-brown and puffed up. Remove from the pan, and drain on soft kitchen paper. Serve as soon as possible after cooking.

Pommes Dauphine

Pommes Duchesse

Pommes Duchesse

(Duchesse Potatoes)

MAKES 450g/1lb (approx)

Metric/imperial		American
450g/1 lb	old potatoes	1 lb
25g/1 oz	butter	2 tablespoons
	1 egg	
	salt, freshly ground pepper	
	a little ground nutmeg	
	beaten egg	

Boil or steam the potatoes, then drain thoroughly, peel and sieve. Beat in the butter and egg, and season to taste with salt, pepper and the nutmeg.

Using a forcing (pastry) bag with a large rose nozzle (tube), pipe pyramids of potato on to a greased baking sheet. Brush with a little beaten egg, and bake in a fairly hot oven, 200°C/400°F/Gas 6, for about 15 minutes or until the potatoes are a good golden-brown.

Gratin Dauphinois

(Potato and Cheese Bake)

SERVES 6

Metric/imperial		American
900g/2 lb	potatoes, peeled and thinly sliced	2 lb
	1 large onion, thinly sliced	
25g/1 oz	butter	2 tablespoons
225g/8 oz	Gruyère cheese, grated	2 cups
	salt, freshly ground pepper	
	ground nutmeg	
150ml/¼ pint	single (light) cream	⅔ cup

Blanch the potatoes and onion for 30 seconds in boiling water, then drain. Put a layer of potatoes in the bottom of a greased casserole, dot with a little of the butter, and sprinkle with some of the onion and cheese, a little salt, pepper and the nutmeg. Pour over some of the cream. Repeat the layers until all the ingredients have been used, finishing with a layer of cheese. Pour the remaining cream on top. Cover and bake in a fairly hot oven, 190°C/375°F/Gas 5, for 1 hour. Remove from the oven, and place under a hot grill (broiler) for 5 minutes or until the top of the cheese is golden-brown and bubbling.

Petits Pois à la Française

(Peas Cooked with Lettuce)

SERVES 6

Metric/imperial		American
50g/2 oz	butter	¼ cup
	1 lettuce heart, shredded	
	1 bunch of spring onions (scallions), chopped	
675g/1½ lb	fresh shelled peas	1½ lb
	salt, freshly ground pepper	
	a pinch of sugar	

Melt the butter in a pan, add the lettuce, spring onions (scallions), peas, seasoning and sugar, then cover and simmer gently for 20–25 minutes or until the peas are very tender. Season to taste before serving.

Purée de Carottes et de Piments Doux

(Carrot and Red Pepper Purée)

Metric/imperial		American
675g/1½ lb	carrots, cut into pieces	1½ lb
	chicken stock	
	salt, freshly ground pepper	
	1 large red pepper, skinned, halved and de-seeded	
25g/1 oz	butter	2 tablespoons
75g/3 oz	shallots, finely chopped	¾ cup
	1 clove of garlic, crushed	
	a pinch of ground ginger	
3 × 15ml spoons/ 3 tablespoons	double (heavy) cream	4 tablespoons
	1 egg yolk	
	2 medium red peppers, halved lengthways and de-seeded	
	GARNISH finely chopped red pepper or paprika	

Cook the carrots gently in the chicken stock with seasoning to taste until tender, then drain. Purée the cooked carrots with the red pepper and salt and pepper to taste in a blender or food processor; alternatively, pass through a sieve until smooth.

Melt the butter in a pan, and cook the shallots gently for 3 minutes. Add the garlic, and cook for a further minute. Add the carrot and red pepper purée, and stir over gentle heat until the excess moisture evaporates. Add a little ground ginger to taste, then beat together the cream and egg yolk, and add to the purée. Keep warm.

Blanch the medium peppers in boiling water for 3–4 minutes, then drain thoroughly. Put a red pepper shell on to each plate, and fill with the hot purée. Garnish with a little finely chopped pepper or with paprika.

Serve either as an accompanying vegetable or as a separate vegetable course.

Purée de Carottes et de Piments Doux

Ratatouille

Metric/imperial		American
4 × 15ml spoons/ 4 tablespoons	olive oil	5 tablespoons
225g/8 oz	onions, sliced	½ lb
	1 clove of garlic, crushed	
50g/2 oz	red pepper, de-seeded and cut into strips	⅓ cup
50g/2 oz	green pepper, de-seeded and cut into strips	⅓ cup
225g/8 oz	aubergine (eggplant), cut into 1.25cm/½ inch slices	½ lb
225g/8 oz	courgettes (zucchini), cut into 1.25cm/½ inch slices	½ lb
450g/1 lb	tomatoes, skinned and roughly chopped	1 lb
	salt, freshly ground pepper	
1 × 2.5ml spoon/ ½ teaspoon	coriander seeds	½ teaspoon

Heat the oil in a pan and gently fry the onions, garlic and red and green pepper for about 10 minutes. Add the remaining oil, the aubergine (eggplant) and the courgettes (zucchini). Cover and simmer gently for 30 minutes, stirring occasionally to prevent the vegetables from sticking to the bottom. Add the tomatoes, seasoning and the coriander seeds, and simmer for a further 15 minutes. Serve hot or cold.

Ratatouille

Croustades aux Asperges

(Asparagus Croustades)

SERVES 6–8

Metric/imperial		American
	6–8 small French rolls	
	50 heads asparagus, cooked	
	1 egg, beaten	
300ml/½ pint	Sauce Béchamel (page 75)	1¼ cups
	salt, freshly ground pepper	
1 × 5ml spoon/ 1 teaspoon	strained lemon juice	1 teaspoon

Cut off the tops of the rolls and scoop out the soft crumb inside. Put the rolls, together with the tops, on a baking sheet, and put into a hot oven, 220°C/425°F/Gas 7, for 5 minutes or until they are very crisp.

Cut off the asparagus points, and keep warm. Either rub the stalks through a sieve, or trim off and discard all the inedible parts of the stems and process the rest in a blender or food processor to give a smooth purée. Mix together the egg, sauce and the asparagus purée, put over gentle heat, season well and add the lemon juice.

Spoon the sauce into the hot rolls, garnish with the asparagus points, and replace the tops on the rolls. Serve at once.

Serve as a separate vegetable course.

Carottes Rapées

(Grated Carrot Salad)

Metric/imperial		American
	4 medium carrots, grated	
	2 shallots, chopped	
	sauce vinaigrette (page 78)	
	French (Dijon-style) mustard	
2 × 15ml spoons/ 2 tablespoons	chopped fennel and parsley, mixed	3 tablespoons
	GARNISH chopped fennel	
	chopped parsley	

Mix the carrots with the shallots, sauce and the mustard. Fold in the chopped fennel and parsley, and chill until required.

Drain off any surplus liquid, and serve garnished with more chopped herbs.

Tomates Farcies à la Provençale

(Stuffed Tomates Provençale)

Metric/imperial		American
	8 medium tomatoes, halved crossways and de-seeded	
	salt, freshly ground pepper	
1 × 15ml spoon/ 1 tablespoon	olive oil	1 tablespoon
50g/2 oz	shallots, finely chopped	½ cup
	1 small clove of garlic, crushed	
25g/1 oz	butter	2 tablespoons
75g–100g/3–4 oz	fresh white breadcrumbs	1½–2 cups
1 × 15ml spoon/ 1 tablespoon	fresh parsley, chopped	1 tablespoon

Place the tomatoes in an ovenproof dish, and season lightly with salt and pepper. Heat the oil in a pan and fry the shallots and garlic gently without browning. Add the butter, and heat until melted, then add the breadcrumbs and parsley. Season to taste, and mix together well. Spoon into the tomato halves, and bake in a hot oven, 220°C/425°F/Gas 7, for 15 minutes or until the breadcrumbs are lightly browned.

Salade de Tomates

(Tomato Salad)

SERVES 4–6

Metric/imperial		American
	1 clove of garlic, cut in half	
450g/1 lb	tomatoes, skinned and sliced	1 lb
	salt, freshly ground pepper	
25g/1 oz	stoned black (pitted ripe) olives	scant ¼ cup
3 × 15ml spoons/ 3 tablespoons	sauce vinaigrette (page 78)	4 tablespoons
1 × 5ml spoon/ 1 teaspoon	fresh basil, chopped	1 teaspoon

Rub a salad bowl with the garlic, then place the tomatoes in the bowl, and season lightly with salt and pepper. Add the olives, and pour over the sauce. Sprinkle with the chopped basil before serving.

Salade Champenoise

Place the vegetables in layers in a large salad bowl or in four glasses. Pour the champagne over them, then leave to stand, covered, for 15–20 minutes.

To make the dressing, stir the vinegar, oil, salt and pepper into the anchovy fillets.

Just before serving, pour the brandy over the salad, then pour over the dressing.

Salade D'Aubergines et D'Oranges

(Aubergine and Orange Salad)

SERVES 4–6

Metric/imperial		American
	2 medium aubergines (eggplants), cut into 2.5cm/1 inch cubes	
	salt, freshly ground pepper	
6 × 15ml spoons/ 6 tablespoons	olive oil	7 tablespoons
175g/6 oz	shallots, finely chopped	1½ cups
	1 clove of garlic, crushed	
	finely grated rind of ½ orange	
6 × 15ml spoons/ 6 tablespoons	dry white wine	7 tablespoons
	GARNISH orange segments	
	strips of orange rind	
	sprigs fresh dill	

Put the aubergine (eggplant) pieces into a colander and sprinkle generously with salt. Leave to drain for 30 minutes, then pat dry on soft kitchen paper. Heat 2 × 15ml spoons/ 2 tablespoons/3 US tablespoons oil in a pan, and fry the shallots gently for 3 minutes. Add the garlic, and fry gently for another minute. Add the remaining oil, then add the aubergines (eggplant), and fry gently for 3–4 minutes. Add the orange rind, white wine and salt and pepper to taste, then simmer gently until the aubergine (eggplant) cubes are just tender. Leave to cool, then chill.

Spoon on to four small serving plates, leaving the edge of the plate free. Border one section of each plate with orange segments, and garnish with strips of orange rind and feathery pieces of dill.

Salade Champenoise

(Mixed Vegetable Salad with Champagne)

Metric/imperial		American
450g/1 lb	potatoes, cooked and sliced	1 lb
450g/1 lb	cooked French (green) beans, cut into 2.5cm/1 inch lengths	1 lb
225g/8 oz	small young (early) carrots, coarsely grated	1½ cups
100g/4 oz	stoned black (pitted ripe) olives	¾ cup
300ml/½ pint	dry champagne	1¼ cups
4 × 5ml spoons/ 4 teaspoons	brandy	4 teaspoons
	DRESSING vinegar	
2 × 5ml spoons/ 2 teaspoons	vinegar	2 teaspoons
4 × 5ml spoons/ 4 teaspoons	oil	4 teaspoons
	salt, freshly ground pepper	
	4 anchovy fillets, finely chopped	

DESSERTS

Babas au Rhum

(Rum Babas)

MAKES 12

Metric/imperial		American
5 × 15ml spoons/ 5 tablespoons	**milk**	6 tablespoons
15g/½ oz *or* 2 × 5ml spoons/2 teaspoons	**fresh (compressed) yeast** or **dried yeast**	½ cake or 2 teaspoons
175g/6 oz	**strong white (hard-wheat** or **unbleached) flour**	1½ cups
½ × 2·5ml spoon/ ¼ teaspoon	**salt**	¼ teaspoon
2 × 5ml spoons/ 2 teaspoons	**sugar**	2 teaspoons
75g/3 oz	**butter**	6 tablespoons
	3 eggs	
675g/1½ lb (approx)	**prepared fresh** or **canned fruit**	1½ lb (approx)
150ml/¼ pint	**double (heavy) cream**	⅔ cup
	RUM SYRUP	
75g/3 oz	**lump sugar**	6 tablespoons
150ml/¼ pint	**water**	⅔ cup
2 × 15ml spoons/ 2 tablespoons	**rum**	3 tablespoons
1 × 15ml spoon/ 1 tablespoon	**lemon juice**	1 tablespoon

Warm the milk until tepid. Blend in the fresh (compressed) yeast or sprinkle on the dried yeast. Stir in 25g/1 oz/¼ US cup of the flour, and leave in a warm place for 20 minutes. Sift the rest of the flour, the salt and the sugar into a bowl, then rub (cut) in the butter. Add the yeast, then add the eggs, and beat until well mixed.

Pour half the mixture into 12 greased baba tins, cover with a large, lightly oiled polythene (plastic) bag, and leave in a warm place for about 20 minutes or until they are two-thirds full. Bake in a fairly hot oven, 200°C/400°F/Gas 6, for 10–15 minutes or until golden-brown and springy to the touch.

To make the rum syrup, put the sugar and water in a pan, and heat until the sugar has dissolved. Bring to the boil and boil steadily for 8 minutes, then add the rum and lemon juice.

Turn the warm rum babas on to a serving dish, prick all over with a fine skewer, and spoon the rum over them. Fill with the fruit, and decorate with the cream.

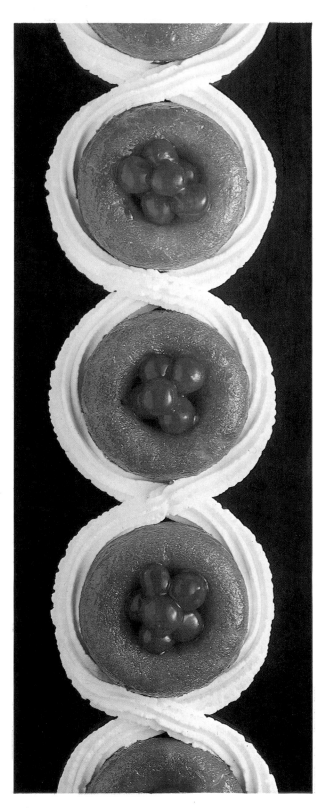

Babas au Rhum

Savarin

SERVES 6–8

Metric/imperial		American
5 × 15ml spoons/ 5 tablespoons	milk	6 tablespoons
15g/½ oz *or* 2 × 5ml spoons/2 teaspoons	fresh (compressed) yeast or dried yeast	½ cake or 2 teaspoons
175/6 oz	strong white (hardwheat or unbleached) flour	1½ cups
½ × 2.5ml spoon/ ¼ teaspoon	salt	¼ teaspoon
2 × 5ml spoons/ 2 teaspoons	sugar	2 teaspoons
75g/3 oz	butter	6 tablespoons
	3 eggs	
	RUM SYRUP	
75g/3 oz	lump sugar	6 tablespoons
150 ml/¼ pint	water	⅔ cup
2 × 15ml spoons/ 2 tablespoons	rum	3 tablespoons
1 × 15ml spoon/ 1 tablespoon	lemon juice	1 tablespoon
	GLAZE	
3 × 15ml spoons/ 3 tablespoons	apricot jam	4 tablespoons
2 × 15ml spoons/ 2 tablespoons	water	3 tablespoons

Warm the milk until tepid. Blend in the fresh (compressed) yeast or sprinkle on the dried yeast. Stir in 25g/1 oz/¼ US cup of the flour and leave in a warm place for 20 minutes. Sift the rest of the flour, the salt and the sugar into a bowl, then rub (cut) in the butter. Add the yeast, then add the eggs, and beat until well mixed.

Pour the mixture into an oiled 20 cm/8 inch ring mould, cover with a large, lightly oiled polythene (plastic) bag, and leave in a warm place until the mixture has almost reached the top of the tin. Bake in a fairly hot oven, 200°C/400°F/ Gas 6, for about 20 minutes or until golden-brown and springy to the touch.

To make the rum syrup, put the sugar and water in a pan and heat until the sugar has dissolved. Bring to the boil and boil steadily for 8 minutes, then add the rum and lemon juice.

Turn the warm savarin on to a serving dish, prick all over with a fine skewer, and spoon the rum syrup over it.

To make the glaze, sieve the apricot jam into a saucepan, add the water, and bring to the boil, stirring all the time. Brush the glaze all over the soaked savarin.

Crème Brûlée

Metric/imperial		American
300ml/½ pint	single (light) cream	1¼ cups
300ml/½ pint	double (heavy) cream)	1¼ cups
	6 egg yolks	
75g/3 oz (approx)	caster sugar	7 tablespoons (approx)
1 × 15ml spoon/ 1 tablespoon	brandy	1 tablespoon

Warm the creams together slowly in a double boiler or a basin (heatproof mixing bowl) over a pan of hot water. Beat together thoroughly the egg yolks and 25g/1 oz/2 US tablespoons of the caster sugar. When the cream feels just warm to the finger, pour it on to the yolks, stir and return to the double saucepan. Continue to cook gently for about 40 minutes, stirring all the time with a wooden spoon until the custard thickens to the consistency of single (light) cream. Scrape down the sides of the pan frequently to prevent lumps forming, and do not let the custard come near boiling point. Add the brandy, then strain the custard into four shallow flameproof dishes, and stand them on a baking sheet. Bake in a warm oven, 160°C/325°F/Gas 3, for 5–10 minutes until a skin has formed on the top of each. Do not allow them to colour. Leave to cool, then chill in a refrigerator for at least 3–4 hours, or preferably overnight.

Sprinkle the remaining caster sugar over the surface of each custard to cover it entirely with an even, thin layer. Place under a hot grill (broiler) for 10–15 minutes or until the sugar melts and turns to caramel. Keep the top of the custard about 10cm/4 inches from the heat. Serve hot or cold.

If serving cold, tap the caramel sharply with the back of a spoon to break it up.

Charlotte Russe

Charlotte Russe

SERVES 6–8

Metric/imperial		American
600ml/1 pint	prepared lemon jelly (lemon-flavored gelatin) (see Note)	2½ cups
	glacé (candied) cherries	
	angelica	
	24 sponge (lady) fingers	
	4 egg yolks	
75g/3 oz	sugar	6 tablespoons
600ml/1 pint	milk	2½ cups
1 × 5ml spoon/ 1 teaspoon	vanilla essence (extract)	1 teaspoon
25g/1 oz	gelatine (unflavored gelatin)	4 envelopes
4 × 15ml spoons/ 4 tablespoons	water	5 tablespoons
300ml/½ pint	double (heavy) cream	1¼ cups

Pour half the jelly into a 2.4 litre/4 pint/5 US pint Charlotte Russe mould or cake tin (pan). When nearly set, arrange the cherries and angelica in a pattern on the jelly. Cover with a little more jelly, and leave to set. Leave the remaining jelly to set.

Arrange the sponge (lady) fingers around the sides of the mould, fitting them as closely together as possible.

Beat together the yolks and sugar until thick and creamy. Heat the milk gently, pour on to the mixture, stir well, and flavour with vanilla essence (extract). Strain back into the saucepan, and cook over gentle heat until the custard thickens slightly.

Soften the gelatine in the water in a heatproof container, then stand the container in a pan of hot water, and stir until the gelatine has dissolved. Cool until tepid, then add to the custard, and leave until cold.

Whip the cream until stiff, and fold three-quarters of it into the custard mixture. Spoon into the prepared mould, and leave to set, preferably overnight.

Trim the upper ends of the sponge (lady) fingers to the level of the filling. Unmould the Charlotte Russe by dipping the base of the mould in and out of hot water for a few seconds, then invert it on to a serving dish. Chop the remaining jelly with a hot knife, and arrange around the dish. Pipe the remaining whipped cream in rosettes around the outer edge of the Charlotte Russe.

Note The jelly (gelatin) should still be liquid.

Profiteroles au Chocolat

SERVES 8

Metric/imperial		American
300ml/½ pint	water	1¼ cups
50g/2 oz	butter	¼ cup
	a pinch of salt	
100g/4 oz	flour, sifted	1 cup
	1 egg yolk	
	2 eggs	
300ml/½ pint	Crème Chantilly (page 79)	1¼ cups
	CHOCOLATE GLACÉ ICING	
100g/4 oz	plain (semi-sweet) chocolate, grated	4 squares
2 × 15ml spoons/ 2 tablespoons	water	3 tablespoons
4 × 5ml spoons/ 4 teaspoons	softened butter	4 teaspoons
225g/8 oz	icing (confectioner's) sugar, sifted	1¾ cups

Put the water, butter and salt in a saucepan, and bring to the boil. Remove from the heat and add the flour all at once. Return to the heat and beat well with a wooden spoon until the mixture forms a smooth paste which leaves the sides of the pan clean. Remove from the heat, cool, slightly, add the egg yolk, and beat well. Add the whole eggs, one at a time, beating thoroughly between each addition.

Put the mixture in a forcing (pastry) bag with a 2·5cm/1 inch nozzle (tube), and pipe 24–30 small choux on to a lightly greased baking sheet. Bake in a hot oven, 220°C/425°F/Gas 7, for 30 minutes. Reduce the heat to moderate, 180°C/350°F/Gas 4, and bake for a further 10 minutes. Remove the choux from the oven, open them at the bottom, remove any uncooked paste, and leave to dry out and cool completely.

To prepare the glacé icing, gently warm the chocolate, water and butter in a small pan, stirring constantly until the mixture is smooth and creamy. Stir in the icing (confectioner's) sugar, a little at a time, adding a little extra water if necessary to make a coating consistency.

Fill the cold choux buns with the *Crème Chantilly*, and glaze the tops with the glacé icing, reserving some for assembling the dish. Let the icing harden, then arrange the choux in a pyramid – this is easiest done if they can be arranged against the sides of a conical mould. Stick them together with small dabs of reserved icing.

Serve three or four choux per person, with hot *Sauce Chocolat* (page 79).

Crème Caramel

Metric/imperial		American
100g/4 oz	lump sugar	½ cup
150ml/¼ pint	water	⅔ cup
300ml/½ pint	milk	1¼ cups
100ml/4 fl oz	single (light) cream	½ cup
	2 eggs	
	2 egg yolks	
25g/1 oz	caster sugar	2 tablespoons
	a few drops vanilla essence (extract)	

Prepare a thickly folded band of newspaper long enough to encircle a 12.5cm/5 inch round cake tin (pan) or charlotte mould. Heat the tin or mould in boiling water or in the oven and wrap the newspaper round it.

Prepare the caramel by heating the sugar and water together, stirring occasionally, until the sugar dissolves completely. Bring to the boil gently, then boil, without stirring, for about 10 minutes until the syrup turns golden-brown. Do not let it turn dark brown as it will have a bitter taste. Pour the caramel into the warmed, dry tin, tilt and turn it, holding it by the paper, until the base and sides are evenly coated. Leave until cold and set.

Warm the milk and cream to approximately 65°C/149°F; do not let it come near the boil. Beat together the whole eggs, egg yolks and sugar, and stir in the milk. Add a few drops of vanilla essence (extract). Strain the custard into the tin or mould, stand it in a shallow tin (pan) containing enough warm water to come half-way up the sides of the dish, and bake in a very cool–cool oven, 140–150°C/ 275–300°F/Gas 1–2, for 1 hour.

Remove the cooked custard and leave for a few minutes, then turn it out carefully on to a warmed dish. The caramel will run off and serve as a sauce. Break up the reserved caramel by tapping sharply with a metal spoon. Decorate the top of the custard with the pieces of broken caramel.

Coeur à la Crème

Coeur à la Crème

(Fruit Cheese)

Metric/imperial		American
350g/12 oz	curd cheese, sieved	1½ cups
75g/3 oz	caster sugar	6 tablespoons
	finely grated rind of ½ lemon	
	SAUCE 2 large ripe peaches, skinned, halved, stoned (pitted) and chopped	
	juice of ½ lemon	
4 × 15ml spoons/ 4 tablespoons (approx)	dry white wine	5 tablespoons (approx)
2 × 15ml spoons/ 2 tablespoons	Grand Marnier	3 tablespoons
	DECORATION 4 ripe strawberries, sliced into fans	

Beat the cheese until smooth with the sugar and lemon rind. Press into four small pots or moulds, preferably with perforated bases. Chill for 4–6 hours.

To make the sauce, blend the peaches with the lemon juice and white wine until smooth, then add the Grand Marnier. If the sauce seems too thick, add a little extra wine.

Unmould each set 'cheese' on to a small plate, and spoon the peach sauce around the base. Arrange a strawberry fan on top of each one, and position the stalk decoratively.

Soufflé au Grand Marnier

SERVES 6–8

Metric/imperial		American
225g/8 oz	sugar	1 cup
150ml/¼ pint	water	⅓ cup
7½ × 15ml spoons/ 7½ tablespoons	gelatine (unflavored gelatin)	8½ tablespoons
	7 eggs, separated	
300ml/½ pint	double (heavy) cream	1¼ cups
	juice of 1 lemon	
150ml/¼ pint	Grand Marnier	⅔ cup
	2 macaroons, crushed	

Dissolve the sugar and 4 × 15ml spoons/4 tablespoons/5 US tablespoons of the water over low heat, then bring to the boil, and boil to the soft ball stage (115°C/239°F).

Soften the gelatine in the remaining water in a heatproof container, then stand the container in a pan of hot water, and stir until the gelatine has dissolved.

Pour the dissolved sugar on to the egg yolks, then add the gelatine, beating until the mixture is cold and fluffy. Whip the cream until it holds its shape, then fold into the egg mixture with the lemon juice and Grand Marnier. Whisk the egg whites until firm, then fold them in gently just before the mixture sets. Pour into a prepared 600ml/1 pint/ 2½ US cup soufflé dish, then chill. Press the macaroon crumbs into the sides and top of the soufflé before serving.

Vacherin de Framboise

(Raspberry Meringue Gâteau)

Metric/imperial		American
	3 egg whites	
175g/6 oz	caster sugar	¾ cup
300ml/½ pint	double (heavy) cream	1¼ cups
1 × 5ml spoon/ 1 teaspoon	caster sugar	1 teaspoon
	Kirsch	
350g/12 oz	fresh raspberries	¾ lb
	DECORATION angelica leaves	

Line two baking sheets with greaseproof (waxed) paper. Draw a 15cm/6 inch circle on each one and very lightly oil the paper.

Whisk together the egg whites and sugar in a basin (heatproof mixing bowl) over a pan of gently simmering water until the mixture is very thick and holds its shape. Put into a forcing (pastry) bag with a 1.25cm/½ inch plain nozzle (tube), and starting from the middle of one circle, pipe round and round on to one baking sheet, to form a coiled, flat round 15cm/6 inch in diameter. Pipe a similar round on the other sheet. Use any remaining mixture to pipe small meringue shells. Bake in a very cool oven, 110°C/225°F/ Gas ¼, for 1–1½ hours, then leave to cool.

Whip the cream until it is thick and stands in firm peaks, then stir in the 1 × 5ml spoon/1 teaspoon caster sugar and Kirsch to taste.

Place one of the meringue rounds on a serving plate, spread with some of the cream, and arrange half the raspberries on it in a flat layer. Put the second meringue on top of the raspberries, arrange the rest of the raspberries in the centre, and pipe a decorative edge of cream round the berries. Decorate the sides of the vacherin with the small meringues and with angelica leaves.

Sorbet aux Brugnons

(Nectarine Sorbet)

SERVES 6

Metric/imperial		American
	4 large ripe nectarines, skinned, halved, stoned (pitted) and chopped	
450ml/¾ pint	water	2 cups
150ml/¼ pint	dry white wine	⅔ cup
175g/6 oz	sugar	¾ cup
	2 egg whites	
300ml/½ pint	single (light) cream	1¼ cups
1–2 × 15ml spoons/ 1–2 tablespoons	Cointreau	1–3 tablespoons
	DECORATION matchstick strips of orange rind	

Put the chopped nectarines into a pan with the water, and simmer until tender. Pass through a sieve or process in a blender or food processor until smooth. Return to the pan and add the white wine. Add the sugar, and stir until dissolved. Boil for 2–3 minutes, then pour into a shallow container, and freeze until slushy.

Whisk the egg whites until stiff but not dry, then fold lightly but thoroughly into the semi-frozen sorbet (sherbet). Return to the freezer until firm.

To serve, mix together the cream and Cointreau, then scoop the sorbet (sherbet) on to small flat dishes, surround each portion with the Cointreau-flavoured cream, and decorate with strips of orange rind.

Sorbet aux Brugnons

Petits Pots au Chocolat

(Chocolate Creams)

SERVES 6

Metric/imperial		American
150ml/¼ pint	milk	⅔ cup
4 × 15ml spoons/ 4 tablespoons	caster sugar	5 tablespoons
	a pinch of salt	
100g/4 oz	plain (semi-sweet) chocolate, coarsely grated	4 squares
100g/4 oz	unsalted butter, chopped	½ cup
	8 egg yolks	

Warm the milk, sugar and salt in a small saucepan, and stir until the sugar dissolves. Put to one side.

Put the chocolate and butter into a large basin (heatproof mixing bowl) and stand it over a pan of hot water. Heat gently until melted, stirring all the time. When the mixture is quite smooth, add the milk, and mix it in thoroughly. Using a balloon whisk if possible, beat in the egg yolks, one at a time; on no account let them curdle. Pour into six small pots or ramekin dishes, and chill well before serving.

Clafouti aux Cerises

(Cherry Batter Pudding)

SERVES 6

Metric/imperial		American
4 × 5ml spoons/ 4 teaspoons	lard (shortening)	4 teaspoons
4 × 5ml spoons/ 4 teaspoons	butter	4 teaspoons
	2 eggs	
	1 egg yolk	
75g/3 oz	sugar	6 tablespoons
200ml/⅓ pint	milk	⅞ cup
100g/4 oz	flour, sifted	1 cup
	a pinch of ground cinnamon	
450g/1 lb	Morello cherries, drained	1 lb
25g/1 oz	caster sugar	2 tablespoons
1 × 15ml spoon/ 1 tablespoon	Kirsch	1 tablespoon

Blend together the lard (shortening) and butter and use to grease a fluted metal brioche or cake mould about 17.5cm/ 7 inches in diameter (10cm/4 inches at the base).

Beat together the whole eggs, egg yolk and sugar until fluffy and light. Heat the milk until steaming. Gradually blend the flour into the egg mixture alternately with a little of the milk, to make a batter. Blend in the remaining milk, and flavour with cinnamon.

Pour a thin layer of batter into the prepared mould, and bake for 5–7 minutes in a fairly hot oven, 200°C/400°F/ Gas 6, to set the batter. Pour the remaining batter into the mould, add the cherries, and sprinkle with caster sugar. Bake in a fairly hot oven, 200°C/400°F/Gas 6, for 10 minutes, then reduce the heat to 190°C/375°F/Gas 5, and bake for a further 20 minutes. The bottom should be crusty and the top soft like confectioner's custard. Serve warm, sprinkled with the Kirsch.

Oeufs à la Neige

(Poached Meringues with Custard)

Metric/imperial		American
	3 eggs, separated	
225g/8 oz	caster sugar	1 cup
600ml/1 pint	milk	2½ cups
	a few drops vanilla essence (extract)	

Whisk the egg whites until very stiff, then fold in 175g/6 oz/¾ US cup sugar. Pour the milk into a frying pan (skillet) and add a few drops of vanilla essence (extract). Heat gently until the surface of the milk is just shivering. It must not boil or the milk will discolour and form a skin.

Using two dessertspoons (tablespoons), mould egg shapes from the meringue and slide them into the milk. Make only a few at a time, and leave plenty of space between them in the pan as they swell when cooking. Cook slowly for 5 minutes, then turn them over, using a palette knife (metal spatula) and a spoon, and cook for a further 5 minutes. They are very delicate and must be handled with care. Remove from the milk gently, and place on a cloth or soft kitchen paper to drain. Continue making shapes from the meringue and poaching them in the milk, until all the meringue is used. Arrange in a flat serving dish.

Blend the egg yolks with the rest of the sugar, then stir in the milk gradually. Strain the mixture into a saucepan and cook gently, stirring all the time, until the sauce thickens slightly. Do not let it come near the boil or it will curdle. Pour the custard round the meringue, and serve at once.

Gratin de Raisin Noir

Gratin de Raisin Noir

(Gratin of Black Grapes)

SERVES 6

Metric/imperial		American
225g/8 oz	whole black (purple) grapes, skinned and pips removed	½ lb
	4 egg yolks	
100g/4 oz	caster sugar	½ cup
200ml/⅓ pint	double (heavy) cream	⅞ cup
2 × 15ml spoons/ 2 tablespoons	Calvados (applejack)	3 tablespoons
	flaked (slivered) almonds	
	icing (confectioner's) sugar	

Divide the grapes among six lightly greased cocotte dishes (ramekins).

Put the egg yolks and caster sugar into a bowl, and whisk until thick and light. Stand the bowl over a pan of gently simmering water, and add the cream and Calvados (applejack). Whisk the mixture over heat until thick, creamy and greatly increased in volume. Pour this custard over the grapes, leaving a shallow rim at the top. Scatter generously with the almonds and then with icing (confectioner's) sugar. Glaze the tops under a hot grill (broiler). Serve at once accompanied by small *langue du chat* biscuits (cookies).

VARIATION

Frost small clusters of black (purple) grapes with beaten egg white and caster sugar, and use to decorate each dish.

65

Crêpes Suzette

Metric/imperial		American
100g/4 oz	flour	1 cup
½ × 2.5ml spoon/ ¼ teaspoon	salt	¼ teaspoon
	1 egg	
300ml/½ pint	milk	1¼ cups
2 × 15ml spoons/ 2 tablespoons	butter, melted	3 tablespoons
10 × 5ml spoons/ 10 teaspoons	brandy	10 teaspoons
	FILLING	
100g/4 oz	unsalted butter	½ cup
75g/3 oz	caster sugar	6 tablespoons
	grated rind and juice of 1 orange	
1 × 5ml spoon/ 1 teaspoon	lemon juice	1 teaspoon
1 × 15ml spoon/ 1 tablespoon	Grand Marnier	1 tablespoon

Sift the flour and salt into a bowl, then make a well in the centre, and add the egg. Stir in half the milk, gradually working the flour down from the sides. Beat vigorously until the mixture is smooth and bubbly. Stir in the rest of the milk, then beat in the butter.

Heat a little oil in a frying pan (skillet), and pour in 2–3 × 15ml spoons/2–3 tablespoons/3–4 US tablespoons batter, just enough to cover the base of the pan thinly. Tilt and rotate the pan to make sure that the batter runs over the whole surface evenly. Cook over moderate heat for about 1 minute until the pancake is set and golden-brown underneath. Cook the second side for about 30 seconds until golden. Repeat with the rest of the batter, then keep warm.

To make the filling, cream together the butter and sugar, then beat in the orange rind, lemon juice and Grand Marnier. Beat in enough orange juice to give a soft creamy consistency.

Spread the filling over the pancakes, dividing it evenly between them. Fold each one in half, then in half again to make a quarter circle.

Return half the pancakes to the pan and re-heat for 1–2 minutes. As the orange butter melts and runs out, spoon it over the pancakes. Pour in half the brandy, tip the pan to one side, and increase the heat. Ignite the brandy and serve at once with the orange sauce poured over the pancakes. Re-heat and serve the other pancakes in the same way.

Crêpes Suzette

BAKING

Madeleines de Commercy

(Scalloped Sponge Cakes)

MAKES 24

Metric/imperial		American
	cornflour (cornstarch)	
	4 eggs, separated	
100g/4 oz	caster sugar	½ cup
100g/4 oz	flour	1 cup
	a pinch of salt	
100g/4 oz	butter, melted and cooled	½ cup
	2 drops lemon essence (extract)	
	2 drops vanilla essence (extract)	
25g/1 oz	icing (confectioner's) sugar	¼ cup

Grease 24 madeleine moulds (shaped like scallop shells), and dust with cornflour (cornstarch). Whisk the yolks with the sugar until very pale and creamy, then whisk in the flour gradually. Whisk the egg whites with the salt until stiff, then whisk the cooled butter into the cake mixture, and fold in the egg whites at once with the essences (extracts).

Fill the moulds with the mixture, and bake in a fairly hot oven, 190°C/375°F/Gas 5, for 20 minutes. Cool on a wire rack, and dust the ridged sides with icing (confectioner's) sugar before serving.

Madeleines de Commercy

Tuiles aux Amandes

(Almond Biscuits)

Metric/imperial		American
100g/4 oz	sugar	$\frac{1}{2}$ cup
	2 egg whites	
75g/3 oz	flaked blanched (slivered) almonds	$\frac{3}{4}$ cup
25g/1 oz	flour	$\frac{1}{4}$ cup
25g/1 oz	butter, melted	2 tablespoons

Beat together the sugar and egg whites lightly, then fold in the almonds and flour, and add the butter.

Line baking sheets with non-stick baking paper (parchment), and put eight small spoons of the mixture on each one, spreading them out with a knife. Bake in a fairly hot oven, 200°C/400°F/Gas 6, for 10 minutes, then remove them when they are golden-brown at the edges. Press each tuile round a rolling-pin while still hot so that it forms an attractive curved shape.

Gâteau St Honoré

SERVES 10–12

Metric/imperial		American
175g/6 oz	prepared shortcrust (pie) pastry	$\frac{1}{3}$ lb
	beaten egg	
150ml/$\frac{1}{4}$ pint	double (heavy) cream	$\frac{2}{3}$ cup
50g/2 oz	sugar	$\frac{1}{4}$ cup
3 × 15ml spoons/ 3 tablespoons	water	4 tablespoons
	CHOUX PASTRY	
600ml/1 pint	water	$2\frac{1}{2}$ cups
100g/4 oz	butter	$\frac{1}{2}$ cup
	salt	
225g/8 oz	flour, sifted	2 cups
	2 egg yolks	
	4 eggs	
	PASTRY CREAM	
	3 eggs	
50g/2 oz	caster sugar	$\frac{1}{4}$ cup
40g/1$\frac{1}{2}$ oz	flour	6 tablespoons
25g/1 oz	cornflour (cornstarch)	$\frac{1}{4}$ cup
	a few drops vanilla essence (extract)	
300ml/$\frac{1}{2}$ pint	milk	$1\frac{1}{4}$ cups
	DECORATION crystallized (candied) violets	
	crystallized (candied) roses	

Make the choux pastry first. Put the water, butter and salt in a saucepan, and bring to the boil. Remove from the heat and add the flour all at once. Return to the heat and beat well with a wooden spoon until the mixture forms a smooth paste which leaves the sides of the pan clean. Remove from the heat, cool slightly, then add the yolks, and beat well. Add the whole eggs, one at a time, beating thoroughly, between each addition.

Roll out the shortcrust (pie) pastry on a lightly floured surface into a 20cm/8 inch round, and place on a baking sheet. Prick the pastry well and brush with beaten egg. Using a 1.25cm/$\frac{1}{2}$ inch plain nozzle (tube), pipe adjoining buns of choux paste round the edge of the pastry, then brush with beaten egg. Use the remaining choux to pipe 18–20 small choux buns separately. Place the buns on a greased baking sheet, and brush with more beaten egg. Bake in a fairly hot oven, 200°C/400°F/Gas 6, for 15 minutes, then reduce to 190°C/375°F/Gas 5, and bake for a further 10–15 minutes or until the choux are well risen and golden-brown. Cool on a wire rack.

To make the pastry cream, separate two of the eggs. Beat together the yolks, whole egg and the caster sugar. Stir in the flour, cornflour (cornstarch) and the vanilla essence (extract). Heat the milk gently, and gradually beat it into the egg mixture. Return the mixture to the pan, bring to the boil, stirring all the time, and boil for 2–3 minutes. Put the mixture into a clean basin, cover with buttered paper, and leave until cold.

Whip the cream until stiff, then pipe into the choux buns. Put the sugar and water into a small saucepan, heat until the sugar has dissolved, then boil until it is a light straw colour. Remove from the heat.

Dip the bottom of each bun quickly in the syrup, and arrange on the pastry and choux round. Whisk the remaining egg whites until stiff and fold into the pastry cream, with any leftover whipped cream. Fill the centre of the gâteau with the pastry cream. Trickle any remaining caramel on top of the buns, and decorate with crystallized (candied) violets and roses.

Gâteau St Honoré

Bûche de Noël

(Chestnut Christmas Log)

SERVES 6–8

Metric/imperial		American
100g/4 oz	icing (confectioner's) sugar	1 cup
	3 eggs	
4 × 5ml spoons/ 4 teaspoons	rum	4 teaspoons
65g/2½ oz	self-raising (self-rising) flour	½ cup plus 2 tablespoons
	extra icing (confectioner's) sugar	
	FILLING	
900g/2 lb	canned unsweetened chestnut purée	2 lb
300g/11 oz	softened butter	1 cup plus 6 tablespoons
100g/4 oz	caster sugar	½ cup
2 × 15ml spoons/ 2 tablespoons	rum	3 tablespoons
	DECORATIONS marrons glacés or glacé (candied) cherries and angelica	

Grease a 35 × 25cm/14 × 10 inch Swiss roll tin (jelly roll pan) and line it with greased paper. Warm a mixing bowl with hot water, then dry it. Sift in the icing (confectioner's) sugar, and break in the eggs. Beat or whisk vigorously for 5–10 minutes until the mixture is very light and fluffy. Add the rum while beating. When the mixture is like meringue, fold in the flour gently. Turn into the prepared tin (pan), and bake in a hot oven, 220°C/425°F/Gas 7, for 7 minutes. Meanwhile, prepare a sheet of greaseproof (waxed) paper 40 × 30cm/16 × 12 inches in size, and dust it with icing (confectioner's) sugar.

Remove the sponge from the oven, loosen the sides from the tin if necessary, and turn it on to the prepared greaseproof (waxed) paper. Peel off the lining paper. Trim the edges of the sponge, if crisp. Roll it up tightly with the greaseproof (waxed) paper into a Swiss roll (jelly roll) shape, beginning either at one long side to make a long thin roll, or at one short end for a thicker, shorter roll. Cool completely.

Meanwhile, prepare the filling. Beat together the purée and butter, then add the sugar and rum.

When the sponge is cold, unroll it carefully. Minor blemishes and cracks do not matter since they will be covered with the butter cream. Cover the underside of the sponge with just over half the filling, spreading it on thickly at the further edge. When covered, re-roll the sponge, and place it on a sheet of greaseproof (waxed) paper, with the cut edge underneath. Cover it with the remaining filling,

either with a knife or using a forcing (pastry) bag with a ribbon nozzle (tube), imitating the knots and grain of wood.

Serve chilled, surrounded by marrons glacés or decorated with glacé (candied) cherries and angelica.

Gâteau Pithiviers

(Almond Cream Gâteau)

SERVES 8–10

Metric/imperial		American
225g/8 oz	prepared puff pastry	½ lb
	beaten egg	
	icing (confectioner's) sugar	
	APRICOT GLAZE	
225g/8 oz	apricot jam	⅔ cup
2 × 15ml spoons/ 2 tablespoons	water	3 tablespoons
	ALMOND CREAM FILLING	
50g/2 oz	butter	¼ cup
50g/2 oz	caster sugar	¼ cup
	1–2 drops almond essence (extract)	
	1–2 drops orange liqueur	
	1 egg	
4 × 15ml spoons/ 4 tablespoons	flour	5 tablespoons
50g/2 oz	ground almonds	½ cup

Make the filling first. Cream together the butter and sugar, then add the essence (extract) and liqueur. Mix in the egg, and blend smoothly. Mix together the flour and ground almonds, then work them into the butter and sugar mixture to make a smooth pastry cream.

To make the glaze, heat the apricot jam and water gently in a saucepan until smooth, then sieve. Bring to the boil, stirring all the time, until thick.

Roll out the pastry on a lightly floured surface and cut into two rounds 17.5cm/7 inches and 20cm/8 inches in diameter. Place the 17.5cm/7 inch round on a wetted baking sheet, and cover with apricot glaze to within 1.25cm/½ inch of the edge. Spread the glaze with the almond cream in an even layer. Moisten the edge of the pastry, and lay the 20cm/8 inch layer on top. Press the edges to seal. Make five curved cuts in the pastry lid, radiating from the centre at equal intervals. Brush the surface with beaten egg. Let the pastry rest for 20 minutes, then bake in a fairly hot oven, 190°C/375°F/Gas 5, for 30 minutes or until the pastry is risen and set. Dust the surface with icing (confectioner's) sugar, and return to the oven for 5 minutes to glaze. Cool on the sheet.

Paris-Brest

(Ring Gâteau with Praline-flavoured Cream)

SERVES 6

Metric/imperial		American
200ml/⅓ pint	water	⅞ cup
40g/1½ oz	butter	3 tablespoons
	a pinch of salt	
75g/3 oz	flour, sifted	¾ cup
	¾ egg yolk	
	1½ eggs	
	beaten egg	
25g/1 oz	flaked (slivered) almonds	¼ cup
	icing (confectioner's) sugar	
	PRALINE CREAM	
100g/4 oz	sugar	½ cup
2 × 15ml spoons/ 2 tablespoons	water	3 tablespoons
50g/2 oz	hazelnuts (filberts), skins removed	½ cup
150ml/¼ pint	double (heavy) cream	⅔ cup
150ml/¼ pint	single (light) cream	⅔ cup

Put the water, butter and salt in a saucepan, and bring to the boil. Remove from the heat and add the flour all at once. Return to the heat and beat well with a wooden spoon until the mixture forms a smooth paste which leaves the sides of the pan clean. Remove from the heat, cool slightly, add the yolk, and beat well. Add the 1½ eggs, separately, beating thoroughly between each addition.

Put the paste into a forcing (pastry) bag with a 1.25cm/ ½ inch nozzle (tube), and pipe a 17.5cm/7 inch ring on a greased baking sheet. Brush the top with beaten egg, then sprinkle liberally with the almonds. Bake in a fairly hot oven, 190°C/375°F/Gas 5, for 30 minutes, then cool on the sheet.

To make the praline cream, heat the sugar and water until the sugar is a light golden-brown. Stir in the nuts, then leave to harden on an oiled marble or metal surface. Crush the cooled praline finely. Whisk the double (heavy) cream until very stiff, then gradually whisk in the single (light) cream, and fold in the praline.

Split the choux ring into two layers, remove any soft filling inside, and fill with the praline-flavoured cream. The cream will stand up above the pastry casing. Gently put the two halves together so that the gâteau is like a sandwich with a very thick filling. Dust the surface with icing (confectioner's) sugar, and serve at once.

Paris-Brest

Mille-Feuille

SERVES 6–8

Metric/imperial		American
350g/12 oz	prepared puff pastry	¾ lb
300ml/½ pint	double (heavy) cream	1¼ cups
100g/4 oz	raspberry jam	⅓ cup
	ICING	
4 × 5ml spoons/ 4 teaspoons	water	4 teaspoons
100g/4 oz	icing (confectioner's) sugar, sifted	1 cup
1 × 2.5ml/ ½ teaspoon	strained lemon juice	½ teaspoon

Roll out the pastry on a lightly floured surface 3mm/⅛ inch thick, and cut into six 15cm/6 inch rounds. Place on wetted baking sheets, prick well and bake in a very hot oven, 230°C/450°F/Gas 8, for 8–10 minutes until crisp and golden-brown. Lift the rounds off carefully and cool on a wire rack.

Whip the cream until thick, and use with the jam to sandwich each layer of pastry.

To make the icing, put 1 × 15ml spoon/1 tablespoon water into a saucepan with the icing (confectioner's) sugar, and add the lemon juice. Warm very gently, and beat well with a wooden spoon. Use to cover the top layer of pastry. Leave until set.

Tarte aux Pommes Normande

(Normandy Apple Tart)

SERVES 6–8

Metric/imperial		American
350g/12 oz	prepared shortcrust (pie) pastry	¾ lb
675g/1½ lb	cooking apples, peeled, cored and sliced	1½ lb
	juice of 1 lemon	
6 × 15ml spoons/ 6 tablespoons	water	7 tablespoons
75g/3 oz	sugar	6 tablespoons
	2 egg yolks	
	2 dessert (eating) apples, halved, cored and sliced (see Note)	
4 × 15ml spoons/ 4 tablespoons	apricot jam	5 tablespoons

Roll out the pastry thinly on a floured surface and use it to line a loose-bottomed fluted flan tin (pie pan), approximately 22.5cm/9 inches in diameter. Bake blind in a fairly hot oven, 200°C/400°F/Gas 6, for 8–12 minutes.

Put the apples into a saucepan with half the lemon juice and 4 × 15ml spoons/4 tablespoons/5 US tablespoons water. Cover and simmer until the apples are soft and pulpy. Leave to cool, then stir in the sugar and egg yolks.

Spoon the cooled apple purée into the pastry case (pie shell), and arrange the sliced dessert (eating) apples on top in concentric circles. Bake in a fairly hot oven, 190°C/375°F/Gas 5, for 40–45 minutes.

Heat the apricot jam and the remaining water gently in a saucepan until smooth, then sieve. Bring to the boil, stirring all the time, then brush the glaze evenly over the top of the tart, and leave until set.

Note Leave the sliced dessert (eating) apples in water and lemon juice until ready to use, then drain.

Brioches

MAKES 22

Metric/imperial		American
450g/1 lb	strong white (hard-wheat or unbleached) flour	4 cups
1 × 5ml spoon/ 1 teaspoon	salt	1 teaspoon
2 × 5ml spoons/ 2 teaspoons	sugar	2 teaspoons
50g/2 oz	butter	¼ cup
25g/1 oz or 1 × 15ml spoon/1 tablespoon	fresh (compressed) yeast or dried yeast	1 cake or generous 1 tablespoon
8 × 5ml spoons/ 8 teaspoons	warm water	8 teaspoons
	2 eggs	
	beaten egg	

Sift the flour, salt and sugar into a large bowl, then rub (cut) in the butter. Blend the fresh yeast into the warm water or reconstitute the dried yeast. Beat the eggs into the yeast liquid, and stir into the flour to form a soft dough. Turn on to a floured surface and knead for about 5 minutes or until the dough is smooth and no longer sticky. Place in a large, lightly oiled polythene (plastic) bag and leave in a warm place for about 45 minutes or until doubled in size.

Knead the dough again until firm, then cut into 22 equal pieces. Cut off one-quarter of each piece used. Form each large piece into a ball, and place in a greased 7.5cm/3 inch brioche or deep bun tin (tartlet pan). Firmly press a hole in the centre of each one, and place the remaining quarter as a knob in the centre. Place the tins on a baking sheet and cover with the polythene (plastic) bag. Leave in a warm place for about 30 minutes or until the dough is light and puffy. Brush with beaten egg, then bake in a very hot oven, 230°C/450°F/Gas 8, for 15–20 minutes until golden-brown.

Brioches

Croissants

Croissants

MAKES 12

Metric/imperial		American
450g/1 lb	**strong white (hard-wheat or unbleached) flour**	4 cups
1 × 5ml spoon/ 1 teaspoon	**salt**	1 teaspoon
100g/4 oz	**lard (shortening)**	$\frac{1}{2}$ cup
25g/1 oz *or* 1 × 15ml spoon/1 tablespoon	**fresh (compressed) yeast** or **dried yeast**	1 cake or generous 1 tablespoon
200ml/$\frac{1}{3}$ pint	**warm water**	$\frac{7}{8}$ cup
	1 egg, beaten	
75g/3 oz	**unsalted butter**	6 tablespoons
	beaten egg	

Sift the flour and salt into a large bowl. Rub in 25g/1 oz/ 2 US tablespoons of the lard (shortening). Blend the fresh yeast into the warm water or reconstitute the dried yeast. Stir the egg and yeast liquid into the flour, and mix to a soft dough. Turn on to a lightly floured surface and knead for about 8 minutes or until the dough is smooth and no longer sticky. Place in a large, lightly oiled polythene (plastic) bag, and leave at room temperature for 15 minutes.

Meanwhile, beat together the rest of the lard (shortening) and the butter until well mixed, then chill. On a lightly floured surface, roll the dough carefully into an oblong 50 × 20cm/20 × 8 inches. Divide the chilled fat into three. Use one-third to dot over the top two-thirds of the dough, leaving a small border clear. Fold the dough into three by bringing up the plain part of it first, then bringing the top, fat-covered third down over it. Seal the edges together by pressing with the rolling-pin. Give the dough a quarter turn, and repeat the rolling and folding twice, using the other two portions of fat. Place the dough in the polythene bag, and leave in a cool place for 15 minutes. Repeat the rolling and folding three more times, then rest the dough in the polythene (plastic) bag in a cool place for a further 15 minutes.

Roll the dough into an oblong 25 × 35cm/10 × 14 inches, then cut it into six 12.5cm/5 inch squares. Cut each square into triangles. Brush the surface with beaten egg, and roll each triangle loosely, towards the point, finishing with the top underneath. Curve into a crescent shape. Place on a greased baking sheet, and brush with beaten egg. Place the sheet in the polythene (plastic) bag again, and leave in a warm place for about 30 minutes or until the dough is light and puffy. Bake in a hot oven, 220°C/425°F/Gas 7, for 15–20 minutes until golden-brown and crisp.

SAUCES AND OTHER BASICS

Sauce Béchamel

(Foundation White Sauce)

MAKES 600ml/1 pint/2½ cups (approx)

Metric/imperial		American
	1 small onion	
	1 small carrot	
	a piece of celery	
600ml/1 pint	milk	2½ cups
	1 bay leaf	
	a few parsley stalks	
	1 sprig of thyme	
	salt	
	1 clove	
	6 white peppercorns	
	1 blade of mace	
50g/2 oz	butter	¼ cup
50g/2 oz	flour	½ cup
4 × 15ml spoons/ 4 tablespoons	single (light) cream	5 tablespoons

Put the vegetables in a pan and heat with the milk, herbs, salt and spices to simmering point. Leave to infuse for 30 minutes. Do not allow to boil. Strain the milk.

Melt the butter in a saucepan, add the flour, and stir until smooth. Cook over gentle heat, without allowing to colour, for 2–3 minutes, stirring until the mixture begins to bubble. Draw the pan off the heat, and gradually add the flavoured milk, stirring to prevent lumps forming. Return to moderate heat, and bring the sauce to the boil, stirring all the time. When the sauce has thickened, simmer for 3–4 minutes, beating briskly. Season to taste with salt. Add the cream to the sauce, just at boiling point, and remove from the heat immediately. Do not let the sauce reboil.

Sauce Espagnole

(Foundation Brown Sauce)

MAKES 300ml/½ pint/1¼ cups (approx)

Metric/imperial		American
50g/2 oz	butter	¼ cup
50g/2 oz	lean raw ham, chopped	¼ cup
	1 small onion, sliced	
	1 small carrot, sliced	
50g/2 oz	mushrooms, sliced	½ cup
50g/2 oz	flour	½ cup
600ml/1 pint	beef stock	2½ cups
	bouquet garni	
	6 black peppercorns	
	1 bay leaf	
1 × 15ml spoon/ 1 tablespoon	concentrated tomato purée (paste)	1 tablespoon
	salt	

Melt the butter in a saucepan and fry the ham for 2–3 minutes. Add the vegetables, and fry very slowly for 8–10 minutes until golden-brown. Add the flour, and stir until smooth. Cook over gentle heat, stirring frequently, for about 10 minutes or until the flour is a rich brown colour. Draw the pan off the heat and gradually add the stock, stirring all the time to prevent lumps forming. Add the bouquet garni, peppercorns and bay leaf. Return to moderate heat and stir until boiling. Half cover the pan, reduce the heat and simmer the sauce gently for 30 minutes. Add the tomato purée (paste), and simmer the sauce for a further 30 minutes. Rub through a sieve, then season to taste with salt. Re-heat before serving.

Sauce Velouté

(Foundation Fawn Sauce)

MAKES 600ml/1 pint/2½ cups (approx)

Metric/imperial		American
50g/2 oz	butter	¼ cup
	6 button mushrooms	
	12 black peppercorns	
	a few parsley stalks	
50g/2 oz	flour	½ cup
600ml/1 pint	chicken stock	2½ cups
	salt, freshly ground pepper	
	lemon juice	
7 × 15ml spoons/ 7 tablespoons	single (light) cream	8 tablespoons

Melt the butter in a saucepan, and add the mushrooms, peppercorns and parsley stalks. Cook gently for 10 minutes, then add the flour, and stir over gentle heat for 2–3 minutes, without allowing it to colour. Draw the pan off the heat and add the stock gradually, stirring well to prevent lumps forming. Return to gentle heat and heat to simmering point, stirring all the time. Simmer for 3–4 minutes. Rub the sauce through a sieve, then season to taste with salt and pepper, and add lemon juice to taste. Re-heat to boiling point, and stir in the cream. Do not reboil. Use at once.

Serve with meat, poultry, fish or vegetable dishes.

Sauce Bigarade

MAKES 300ml/½ pint/1¼ cups (approx)

Metric/imperial		American
	½ Seville orange	
300ml/½ pint	Sauce Espagnole (page 75)	1¼ cups
	juice of ½ lemon	
4 × 15ml spoons/ 4 tablespoons	red wine	5 tablespoons
1 × 5ml spoon/ 1 teaspoon	redcurrant jelly	1 teaspoon
	salt	
	Cayenne pepper	
	sugar	

Pare the orange rind and cut into neat, thin strips. Put them in a saucepan and cover with a little cold water. Heat to simmering point and cook until just tender, then drain. Squeeze the juice from the orange, add to the *Sauce Espagnole* with the orange rind and lemon juice, and re-heat gently. Stir in the wine and the redcurrant jelly, then add salt, Cayenne pepper and sugar to taste.

Serve with roast duck, goose, pork or ham dishes.

Sauce Mornay

MAKES 300ml/½ pint/1¼ cups (approx)

Metric/imperial		American
300ml/½ pint	Sauce Béchamel (page 75)	1¼ cups
	1 egg yolk	
40g/1½ oz	Parmesan and Gruyère cheeses, grated	⅓ cup
4 × 15ml spoons/ 4 tablespoons	single (light) cream	5 tablespoons
	a few grains Cayenne pepper	

Cool the *Sauce Béchamel*, if necessary. Stir a little into the yolk, and blend together. Add to the rest of the sauce. Heat the sauce gently, stirring carefully, to cook the egg yolk; do not let it boil. Stir the cheeses into the sauce, then add the cream, and season with Cayenne pepper.

Serve with fish, chicken, ham, egg or vegetable dishes.

Sauce Béarnaise

MAKES 200ml/⅓ pint/⅞ cup (approx)

Metric/imperial		American
	1 shallot, finely chopped	
1 × 15ml spoon/ 1 tablespoon	fresh tarragon, chopped	1 tablespoon
1 × 15ml spoon/ 1 tablespoon	fresh chervil, chopped	1 tablespoon
	a small piece of bay leaf	
	4 peppercorns, crushed	
4 × 15ml spoons/ 4 tablespoons	wine or tarragon vinegar	5 tablespoons
	2 egg yolks	
100g/4 oz	softened butter	½ cup
	salt, freshly ground pepper	

Put the shallots in a saucepan with the herbs. Add the peppercorns with the vinegar. Heat to boiling point, then boil gently until reduced by half. Leave to cool, then strain. Heat the sauce in a basin (heatproof mixing bowl) placed in a pan of hot water to avoid boiling the sauce. Whisk in the yolks, one at a time, and stir until thickened. Whisk in the butter, adding a small pat at a time. (The sauce should be as thick as mayonnaise.) Season to taste. Serve the sauce, lukewarm, as soon as possible. Keep warm if necessary, over hot water, and re-whisk before serving.

Serve with steaks, shellfish or grilled (broiled) fish, poultry or eggs.

Sauce Suprême

MAKES 300ml/½ pint/1¼ cups (approx)

Metric/imperial		American
300ml/½ pint	Sauce Velouté (page 76)	1¼ cups
2–4 × 15ml spoons/ 2–4 tablespoons	single (light) cream	3–5 tablespoons
	1 egg yolk	
15–25g/½–1 oz	butter	1–2 tablespoons
	ground nutmeg	
	lemon juice	
	salt, freshly ground pepper	

Cool the *Sauce Velouté*, if necessary. Mix the cream and egg yolk, using the larger quantity of cream for a rich sauce. Stir a little of the cooled sauce into the cream and yolk mixture, then add this to the rest of the sauce. Heat gently, stirring carefully, to thicken the egg yolk; do not let it boil. Whisk in the butter, adding a small pat at a time, then add nutmeg, lemon juice and seasoning to taste. Use at once.

Serve with any meat, poultry, fish or vegetable dish.

Sauce Mousseline

MAKES 100ml/4 fl oz/½ cup (approx)

Metric/imperial		American
	2 eggs	
	1 egg yolk	
1 × 15ml spoon/ 1 tablespoon	chicken stock	1 tablespoon
	salt, freshly ground pepper	
	ground nutmeg	
5 × 15ml spoons/ 5 tablespoons	single (light) cream	6 tablespoons
15g/½ oz	butter, diced	1 tablespoon
1 × 15ml spoon/ 1 tablespoon	lemon juice	1 tablespoon

Put all the ingredients except the butter and lemon juice in a basin (heatproof mixing bowl) over a pan of hot water, and whisk until pale, frothy and of a thick, creamy consistency. This will take 8–10 minutes. Remove from the heat and whisk in the butter, then whisk in the lemon juice gradually, mixing well between each addition to prevent the sauce curdling.

Serve at once with fish, poultry or vegetable dishes.

Sauce Chaudfroid

MAKES 450ml/¾ pint/2 cups (approx)

Metric/imperial		American
300ml/½ pint	Sauce Béchamel (page 75)	1¼ cups
150ml/¼ pint	aspic jelly	⅔ cup
2 × 5ml spoons/ 2 teaspoons	gelatine (unflavored gelatin)	2 teaspoons
	salt, freshly ground pepper	
1 × 5ml spoon/ 1 teaspoon	white wine vinegar or lemon juice	1 teaspoon
1 × 15ml spoon/ 1 tablespoon	double (heavy) cream	1 tablespoon

Cool the *Sauce Béchamel* until tepid. Melt the aspic jelly in a basin (heatproof mixing bowl) placed over hot water. Add the gelatine, and continue to stir over heat until the gelatine dissolves. Cool the aspic jelly until tepid, then fold it into the sauce. Season to taste, then add the vinegar or lemon juice. Rub the sauce through a fine sieve, then fold in the cream. Leave to cool completely, but use while still liquid.

Use to mask cold cooked poultry, veal or fish.

Sauce Hollandaise

MAKES 150ml/¼ pint/⅔ cup (approx)

Metric/imperial		American
3 × 15ml spoons/ 3 tablespoons	white wine vinegar	4 tablespoons
	6 peppercorns	
	½ bay leaf	
	1 blade of mace	
	3 egg yolks	
100g/4 oz	softened butter	½ cup
	salt, freshly ground pepper	

Put the vinegar, peppercorns, bay leaf and mace into a small saucepan, and boil rapidly until the mixture is reduced to 1 × 15ml spoon/1 tablespoon. Strain, then leave to cool.

Add the yolks and a nut of butter to the vinegar, and beat well. Heat the sauce in a basin (heatproof mixing bowl) over a pan of hot water to avoid boiling the sauce, beating until thick. Add the rest of the butter, a small pat at a time, beating well between each addition. When all the butter has been added, the mixture should be thick and glossy. Season lightly with salt and pepper, and serve lukewarm.

Serve with poached fish, asparagus or broccoli.

Sauce Bercy

MAKES 300ml/½ pint/1¼ cups (approx)

Metric/imperial		American
	2 shallots, chopped	
4 × 15ml spoons/ 4 tablespoons	white wine	5 tablespoons
300ml/½ pint	Sauce Velouté (page 76)	1¼ cups
25g/1 oz	butter	2 tablespoons
2 × 5ml spoons/ 2 teaspoons	fresh parsley, chopped	2 teaspoons

Put the shallots into a small saucepan with the wine, and cook until the wine is reduced by half. Add the sauce, and re-heat without allowing it to boil. Whisk in the butter, adding a small pat at a time, then add the parsley.

Serve with fish or meat dishes.

Sauce Demi-Glace

MAKES 300ml/½ pint/1¼ cups (approx)

Metric/imperial		American
150ml/¼ pint	juices from roast meat	⅔ cup
300ml/½ pint	Sauce Espagnole (page 75)	1¼ cups

Add the meat juices to the sauce, then heat slowly to boiling point; boil until the sauce is well reduced. Skim off any fat.

Serve with meat or poultry dishes.

Sauce Tartare

MAKES 150ml/¼ pint/⅔ cup (approx)

Metric/imperial		American
1 × 5ml spoon/ 1 teaspoon each	chopped gherkins, chopped olives, chopped capers, chopped parsley and chopped chives	1 teaspoon each
150ml/¼ pint	mayonnaise	⅔ cup
½ × 2.5ml spoon/ ¼ teaspoon	French (Dijon-style) mustard	¼ teaspoon
2 × 5ml spoons/ 2 teaspoons	wine vinegar or lemon juice	2 teaspoons

Fold the chopped ingredients into the mayonnaise with the mustard, then add the vinegar or lemon juice. Leave for at least 1 hour before serving for the flavours to blend.

Serve with grilled (broiled) or fried fish and meat.

Mayonnaise

MAKES 300ml/½ pint/1¼ cups (approx)

Metric/imperial		American
	2 egg yolks	
1 × 2.5ml spoon/ ½ teaspoon	mustard powder	½ teaspoon
1 × 2.5ml spoon/ ½ teaspoon	salt	½ teaspoon
	pepper	
2 × 15ml spoons/ 2 tablespoons	white wine vinegar, tarragon vinegar or lemon juice	3 tablespoons
300ml/½ pint	olive oil	1¼ cups

Blend the yolks in a basin with the mustard, salt, pepper and 1 × 15ml spoon/1 tablespoon of the vinegar or lemon juice. Beat in the oil very gradually, drop by drop, until about half of it has been added and the mixture looks thick and shiny. Add the remaining vinegar or lemon juice when all the oil has been incorporated.

Store the mayonnaise in a covered basin or jar in the least cold part of a refrigerator; if it becomes too cold, it will separate.

Sauce Vinaigrette

MAKES 100ml/4 fl oz/½ cup (approx)

Metric/imperial		American
2–3 × 15ml spoons/ 2–3 tablespoons	olive oil	3–4 tablespoons
	salt, freshly ground pepper	
1 × 15ml spoon/ 1 tablespoon	wine vinegar	1 tablespoon
1 × 5ml spoon/ 1 teaspoon	finely chopped gherkin	1 teaspoon
1 × 5ml spoon/ 1 teaspoon	finely chopped capers	1 teaspoon
1 × 2.5ml spoon/ ½ teaspoon	finely chopped chives	½ teaspoon
1 × 2.5ml spoon/ ½ teaspoon	finely chopped parsley	½ teaspoon
1 × 2.5ml spoon/ ½ teaspoon	finely chopped tarragon	½ teaspoon

Mix together the oil and salt and pepper. Add the vinegar gradually, stirring all the time with a wooden spoon so that an emulsion is formed. Alternatively, put all the ingredients into a small screw-topped jar, and shake vigorously until well blended.

Mix together with the chopped gherkin, capers and herbs, and leave for at least 1 hour before using for the flavours to blend.

Beurre à la Maître D'Hôtel

(Mâitre d'Hôtel Butter)

MAKES 50g/2oz/¼ cup

Metric/imperial		American
	2–4 large sprigs parsley, blanched and finely chopped	
50g/2 oz	softened butter	¼ cup
	salt, freshly ground pepper	
	a few drops lemon juice	

Work the parsley into the butter with the seasonings and lemon juice. Use at once, or pot and chill until required.

Court Bouillon

(Fish Stock)

Metric/imperial		American
	water	
600ml/1 pint	dry white wine or dry (hard) cider for each 1.2 litres/2 pints/ 5 cups water	2½ cups
2 × 15ml spoons/ 2 tablespoons	white wine vinegar for each 1.2 litres/ 2 pints/5 cups water	3 tablespoons
	2 large carrots, sliced	
	2 large onions, sliced	
	2–3 sticks celery, chopped	
	parsley stalks, crushed	
	1 bouquet garni for each 1.2 litres/ 2 pints/5 cups water	
	a few peppercorns	
	salt, freshly ground pepper	

Put the liquids in a large pan, then add the vegetables with the remaining ingredients. Simmer for 30 minutes, leave to cool, then strain and use as required.

Fleurons

puff pastry
beaten egg

Roll out the pastry 5cm/2 inches thick, and cut out circles with a 5cm/2 inch cutter. Move the cutter half-way across each circle and cut it again, making a half-moon and an almond shape. Roll out and re-cut the almond shapes into half-moon shapes, and place on a baking sheet. Brush the tops with beaten egg, and bake in a fairly hot oven, 200°C/400°F/Gas 6, for 8–10 minutes.

Use to garnish dishes in a white or creamy sauce.

Sauce Chocolat

MAKES 175ml/6 fl oz/¾ cup (approx)

Metric/imperial		American
100g/4 oz	plain (semi-sweet) chocolate, broken into pieces	4 squares
225g/8 oz	sugar	1 cup
150ml/¼ pint	black coffee	⅔ cup
	salt	
1 × 2.5ml spoon/ ½ teaspoon	vanilla essence (extract)	½ teaspoon

Put the chocolate into a saucepan with the other ingredients and stir over gentle heat until the chocolate and sugar melt and blend together.

Crème Chantilly

(Chantilly Cream)

MAKES 300ml/½ pint/1¼ cups (approx)

Metric/Imperial		American
300ml/½ pint	double (heavy) cream	1¼ cups
25g/1 oz	caster sugar	2 tablespoons
	vanilla essence (extract)	

Chill the cream for several hours, then whip it lightly. Just before serving, whip in the sugar and a few drops of vanilla essence (extract) to taste.

INDEX

Agneau Reine Claude 34
Almond Biscuits 68
Almond Cream Gâteau 70
Alouettes sans Têtes 32
Alsace Onion Tart 15
Asparagus Croustades 55
Aubergine and Orange Salad 56

Babas au Rhum 57
Beef Bourguignonne 30
Beef Olives 32
Beurre à la Maître d'Hôtel 79
Bifteck a L'Américaine 30
Blanquette de Veau à L'Ancienne 34
Boeuf à la Bourguignonne 30
Boeuf à la Mode 31
Bouillabaisse 10
Brioches 72
Bûche de Noël 70

Canard à L'Orange 42
Carottes Rapées 55
Carrot and Red Pepper Purée 52
Carrot Soup 8
Cassoulet de Toulouse 38
Champignons à la Grecque 11
Chantilly Cream 79
Charlotte Russe 59
Châteaubriand 29
Cheese Pâté 47
Cheese Ramekins 47
Cherry Batter Pudding 64
Chestnut Christmas Log 70
Chicken à la King 41
Chicken Chasseur 40
Chicken in Cider and Cream Sauce 42
Chicken Liver Tartlets 14
Chocolate Creams 64
Choux Pastry with Cheese 48
Clafouti aux Cerises 64
Coeur à la Crème 61
Consommé Royale 10
Coq au Vin 41
Coquilles St Jacques Mornay 26
Court Bouillon 79
Cream of Cauliflower Soup 9
Cream of Sorrel Soup 9
Crème Brûlée 58
Crème Caramel 60
Crème Chantilly 79
Crème Dubarry 9
Crème Vichyssoise 7
Crêpes Suzette 66
Croissants 74
Croque Monsieur 47
Croustades aux Asperges 55

Dauphine Potatoes 51
Deep-fried Strips of Plaice 23
Duchesse Potatoes 51
Duck with Orange 42

Eggs Courtet 46
Eggs in Cocottes 45
Escargots de Bourgogne 12

Filets de Sole au Melon à la Menthe 20
Fillets of Sole with Mint Sauce and Melon 20

Fish Stock 79
Fleurons 79
Fondue Bourguignonne 32
Foundation Brown Sauce 75
Foundation Fawn Sauce 76
Foundation White Sauce 75
Fruit Cheese 61

Garlic Soup 7
Gâteau Pithiviers 70
Gâteau St Honoré 68
Gigot Boulangère 36
Gougère 48
Goujons de Carrelet 23
Grated Carrot Salad 55
Gratin Dauphinois 52
Gratin de Raisin Noir 65
Gratin of Black Grapes 65
Grilled Double Fillet Steak 29
Grilled Lamb with Greengage Sauce 34

Ham and Cheese Sandwich 47
Haricot Bean Stew with Pork and Lamb 38
Herb Omelet 44
Huîtres 12

Lamb Stew with Vegetables 36
Langoustine Provençale 26
Leek Tart 16
Lyonnaise Potatoes 49

Mackerel in Tomato Sauce 24
Madeleines de Commercy 67
Maître d'Hôtel Butter 79
Maquereau Niçoise 24
Marinated Beef Casserole 31
Marinated Mushrooms 11
Mayonnaise 78
Mille-Feuille 71
Mixed Fish Soup 10
Mixed Vegetable Salad with Champagne 56
Moules à la Marinière 27
Mousse au Saumon 12
Mussels with White Wine 27

Navarin d'Agneau Printanier 36
Nectarine Sorbet 62
Normandy Apple Tart 72

Oeufs à la Neige 64
Oeufs Belle Hélène 45
Oeufs Courtet 46
Oeufs en Cocottes 45
Oeufs Parmentier 45
Omelette Fines Herbes 44
Onion Soup 8
Oysters 12

Paris-Brest 71
Parisienne Potatoes 50
Parmentier Eggs 45
Pâté de Fromage 47
Peas Cooked with Lettuce 52
Petits Pois à la Française 52
Petits Pots au Chocolat 64
Pike Dumplings 23
Pipérade Basque 44
Pistou 7
Poached Eggs with Asparagus Sauce 45
Poached Meringues with Custard 64

Pommes Dauphine 51
Pommes Duchesse 51
Pommes Lyonnaise 49
Pommes Parisienne 50
Pot-au-Feu 31
Potage à la Crecy 8
Potato and Cheese Bake 52
Poulet à la King 41
Poulet Chasseur 40
Poulet Vallée D'Auge 42
Profiteroles au Chocolat 60
Purée de Carottes et de Piments Doux 52

Quenelles de Brochet 23
Quiche aux Poireaux 16
Quiche Lorraine 16

Raie au Beurre Noir 21
Ramekins de Fromage 47
Raspberry Meringue Gâteau 62
Ratatouille 54
Red Mullet Baked in Foil 22
Ring Gâteau with Praline-flavoured Cream 71
Roast Leg of Lamb with Baked Potatoes 36
Roujet en Papillote 22
Rum Babas 57

Salade Champenoise 56
Salade d'Aubergines et d'Oranges 56
Salade de Tomates 55
Salade Niçoise 11
Salmon Mousse 12
Sauce Béarnaise 76
Sauce Béchamel 75
Sauce Bercy 78
Sauce Bigarade 76
Sauce Chaudfroid 77
Sauce Chocolat 79
Sauce Demi-Glace 78
Sauce Espagnole 75
Sauce Hollandaise 77
Sauce Mornay 76
Sauce Mousseline 77
Sauce Suprême 77
Sauce Tartare 78
Sauce Velouté 76
Sauce Vinaigrette 78
Savarin 58
Scalloped Sponge Cakes 67
Scallops Mornay 26
Scampi in Tomato and Mushroom Sauce 26
Scrambled Eggs with Vegetables 44
Skate in Black Butter 21
Snails in Garlic Butter 12
Sole Bonne Femme 18
Sole Colbert 21
Sole Véronique 18
Sorbet aux Brugnons 62
Soufflé au Camembert 46
Soufflé au Grand Marnier 61
Soupe à L'Oignon Gratinée 8
Soupe à L'Oseille 9
Steak au Poivre 28
Steak Diane 28
Steak Tartare 30
Stuffed Tomatoes Provençale 55

Tarte à L'Oignon Alsacienne 15
Tarte aux Pommes Normande 72

Tartelettes de Foie de Volaille 14
Tomates Farcies a la Provençale 55
Tomato Salad 55
Tournedos Rossini 29
Tournedos with Pâté and Mushrooms 29
Tranche de Thon à la Concombre 24
Tripe with Pork in Cider 40
Tripes à la Mode de Caen 40
Trout with Almonds 22
Truite aux Amandes 22
Tuiles aux Amandes 68
Tuna and Cucumber in Puff Pastry 24
Turbot Dugléré 23
Turbot with Tomatoes and Onions 23

Vacherin de Framboise 62
Veal Stew with Mushrooms and Onions 34